LIVING *in* VICTORY

Through

the Power

of Mercy

PURE ✝ LIFE
MINISTRIES

STEVE GALLAGHER

Other titles available by Steve Gallagher

At The Altar of Sexual Idolatry
At The Altar Of Sexual Idolatry-Workbook
En El Altar de la Idolatria Sexual
Break Free from the Lusts of this World
The Walk of Repentance
Fork in the Road
How to Run a Successful Support Group

For these books and other teaching
materials about overcoming sexual sin,
contact:
Pure Life Ministries
P.O. Box 410
Dry Ridge, KY 41035
(888) 293-8714 - Order Line
(859) 824-4444 - Office
(859) 824-5159 - FAX
info@purelifeministries.org
www.purelifeministries.org

Advanced Praise for Living in Victory

"Because we have embraced the faulty level of the world, our houses are weak, our churches are vulnerable and our families are falling down all around us. Steve Gallagher's *Living in Victory* takes us back to the only level we should use to build...the Word of God. Be prepared to be uncomfortably challenged as he exposes the faulty levels in your life. At first it will feel like being torn down, but in time you will see that you are being built up to a new life in Christ."

Dannah Gresh
Author of *And the Bride Wore White*
and *Pursuing the Pearl*

"Steve Gallagher's transparent openness about his own shortcomings and inspiring biblical teaching about God's mercy is deeply moving. While reading, I was painfully aware of my own failures in areas of purity, but at the same time encouraged that it is not too late for me. *Living in Victory* gives me hope that a life wholly devoted to God is both doable and necessary. A must-be-read book for any man searching to live a life pleasing to God."

Charlie Hungerford
Assistant Director
University Communications
Drury University

"Steve Gallagher approaches the subject of victorious living not as a self-made man, but as a God-made man—an all-too-fallible man who has placed his fate in the hands of a mighty and gracious God. If you're tired of pat answers and you're ready to let God change you, buy this book!"

David E. Fessenden
Managing Editor
Christian Publications, Inc.

"Steve Gallagher's new book, *Living in Victory,* is a well written and excellent resource for any Christian who wants to live an abundant life, free from the bondage of the flesh. As with his other books, Steve speaks from the heart and easily connects with the reader. This book will be a blessing to many readers."

Nick Harrison
Editor for a major Christian publisher

*To Doug & Millie Detert
who taught me through their own lives
the meaning of God's Mercy.*

Acknowledgements

My sincere appreciation to Charlie Hungerford and Bradley Furges
for their help editing this book.

Table of Contents

Introduction

Living in Victory

Victory...the very word can almost seem like a cruel joke to someone bound up in habitual sin. Most strugglers I know would be thrilled just to live in some degree of liberty from their sexual sin; an abundant spiritual life seeming far-fetched, even ludicrous. My goal is to show the reader that he need not settle for a fear-driven, white-knuckled form of freedom. As a child of God, the bountiful life of victory in Christ is his for the taking!

The problem is convincing a man who has a defeated attitude that he can have so much more than what he has experienced up to this point. It is much the same with trying to tell a man living in the ghetto, making minimum wage, that he should live lavishly. He will look at you as though you have two heads! He has lived in the slums his entire life. He has worked for little pay for years. He might vaguely know that there are those who are wealthy, but that kind of lifestyle is so far from his little world that it is inconceivable that he could ever enjoy it for himself.

Most strugglers would consider themselves victorious if they could find freedom from that one besetting habit. Yet, would that truly make the man victorious? What has really been accomplished if a sex addict no longer frequents massage parlors but is still consumed with lust? Is he truly rich in Christ if he is still selfish, angry and prideful? Does he really know about victorious living if he does not know what it means to live in the power and love of God?

If the man making minimum wage suddenly doubles his pay, it may seem as though he is rich, but it does not make it so. Undoubtedly, his situation has improved. Perhaps he might even be able to move out of the projects and into a better neighborhood.

However, if he wants to become rich, he will have to aspire to more than a raise in pay and a slightly nicer house. He will have to change his entire outlook on life from one of poverty to one of wealth. He will need to become an avid student of the lives of the rich. Most of all, he will need to master the *operating principles of success* that govern the business world.

It is much the same for the person who desires to exchange his defeated spiritual life for one of victory. He too must set his sights much higher than he has in the past. He will also need to study the lives of those who have lived the abundant Christian life. Most of all, he will need to master the *operating principles of success* that open up to him the spiritual fortune available to the believer. Why should any Christian wallow in the ghetto of defeated living when the treasures of Christ are available to him?

The riches, which bring about victorious living, are not the material, temporal trinkets this world system offers, but are found in the unsearchable depths of God Himself. Paul tells us that the Lord is rich in mercy (Ephesians 2:4), and as it turns out, that mercy is the very thing the struggling saint needs.

Everything in the kingdom of God revolves around the love and mercy of the Lord. In fact, His love is the *operating principle* that runs the entire kingdom of God. Jesus expressed this when He said, "'You shall love the Lord your God with all your heart, and with all your soul, and with all your mind.' This is the great and foremost commandment. The second is like it, 'You shall love your neighbor as yourself.' On these two commandments depend the whole Law and the Prophets." In other words, everything that occurs within the realm of God's kingdom revolves around these two principles.

In the same way engineers empower an entire city by harnessing and directing electricity, so too the kingdom of God operates on the power of His love. Mercy is the love of God in action meeting the needs of people. It is a force that continually issues forth from His throne and is directed at those in need.

The secret to victorious living is to tap into God's great

storehouse of mercy for one's own needs and then act as a conduit for that power, directing it toward the lives of others. Overcoming habitual sin is important, but real victory occurs when a person becomes a weapon in the hands of a powerful God against the legions of hell. That is *Living in Victory*!

The first step into that higher life is seeing your need for it.

Part One
Seeing Your Need

Meditation For Today

"Jesus Christ cannot begin to do anything for a man until he knows his need...The entrance into the Kingdom of God is always through the moral frontier of need."[1]

Oswald Chambers

"And my God shall supply all your needs according to His riches in glory in Christ Jesus."[2]

The Apostle Paul

"A man must feel himself in misery, before he will find a remedy; be sick before he will seek a physician; be in prison before he will seek a pardon. A sinner must be weary of his former wicked ways before he will have recourse to Jesus Christ for refreshing. He must be sensible of his spiritual poverty, beggary, and slavery under the devil, before he thirst kindly for heavenly righteousness, and willingly take up Christ's sweet and easy yoke. He must be cast down, confounded, condemned, a cast away, and lost in himself, before he will look about for a Savior."[3]

Robert Bolton

Chapter One

Seeing Your Need

One of my life's greatest blessings is the privilege of working with men who struggle with sexual sin. Over the past 16 years, I have directly or indirectly been involved in the lives of countless men with such problems. I have often pleaded with them, taught them, confronted them, encouraged them, and preached to them in response to their great need to find the Lord. On numerous occasions, I have grieved over their losses, reasoned with them for hours, and agonized in prayer over them. I have tearfully begged them to repent and at times have sternly rebuked those who hesitated or refused to do so. Fortunately, for most of them the negative consequences of their sin opened their eyes and exposed their great need for God to work in their lives.

Whether or not you struggle with sexual sin, you also have a need for God to be greater than He presently is in your life. I say this confidently because it is the need of every human being alive today, whether they are deeply spiritual or completely godless. We all have deep emotional and spiritual needs that can only be met by God and through Him alone. The wonderful news is that God has a universe full of mercy for all of us—mercy to meet our needs, to set us free, and to heal our infirmities, allowing each of us to enter into a life of blessedness. The allocation of this need-fulfilling mercy comes once we begin to see our need for it. The only hindrance to receiving such unmerited favor from Him hinges upon how much we choose to appropriate for ourselves.

This is what I love about working with sexual addicts. Most of them come to Pure Life (a ministry I founded in 1986) because they are in trouble and are desperate for help. Being acutely aware of the absolute necessity of God doing a work inside their hearts and actually acknowledging it, places them into what is an enviable position in the kingdom of God: a man who sees his need.

This is such a tremendous place before the Lord that I often tell these men to thank God for their addiction. If this sounds outrageous to you, consider the following: If Bartimaeus were not blind, would he have been bellowing unashamedly, "Son of David, have mercy on me!" (Mark 10:47)? If the Syro-Phoenician woman's daughter had not been vexed with a devil would she have been willing to "eat of the crumbs which fall from their masters' table" (Matthew 15:27 KJV)? Had King David not been sharply rebuked by Nathan and been forced to see his great crime, would he have ever penned the words, "Have mercy upon me, O God, according to thy lovingkindness: according unto the multitude of thy tender mercies blot out my transgressions" (Psalm 51:1 KJV)? Had Peter not seen how unlike the Lord he was, would he have cried out, "Depart from me, for I am a sinful man, O Lord!" (Luke 5:8)? And finally, if the publican had not seen his great need, would he have "smote upon his breast, saying, God be merciful to me a sinner" (Luke 18:13 KJV)?*

The afflictions and struggles of life are what produce a cry for God's help. Individuals who enjoy a comfortable, smooth ride through life really do not know what it is like to be pressed into a tight place with nowhere or no one to turn to but God. It is only

---

*I do not mean to glorify or justify something as hideous and devilish as a person's obsession with sexual perversion. When you feel the chains of darkness wrapped around your neck you are only looking for one thing: freedom! My point is that the alternative to never having something that compels you to seek God is to be content living with little of His presence in your life. Being freed or healed is wonderful, but the affliction is there to teach us to turn to Him. Having tasted His precious Spirit through the whole ordeal, the person should be like the one leper out of ten who came back and worshipped Him.

human nature for one to "let down" or relax when life becomes more favorable or when certain problems are resolved.

Many men who spend years indulging their sexual appetites only to find themselves in the frightening grip of the devil know what it means to plead for God's mercy. The point of desperation is not some obscure experience with them. It is a very real part of their daily lives. Spiritually bankrupt, they are in such utter despair that their only hope is to find God's way out. Such individuals often have a passion to find the Lord. I know firsthand that freedom from such bondage requires a dogged persistence and genuine zeal to seek after the Lord.

Many who do not know the power of a controlling sin do not seek God with the same degree of fervor. Because their needs are not readily observable, they tend to approach the things of God far more casually. They vaguely understand that God desires to mature and transform them, but they lack an intense craving for any such growth or change. They assume that God will somehow accomplish what is needed in their lives and are content to center their Christian walk on increasing their "head knowledge," naming and claiming this and that, and having occasional spiritual experiences.

Men who really understand their great need for God's work in their lives cannot be satisfied with such a lackadaisical approach. They are in trouble spiritually and have no choice but to find the answer in God no matter what the cost.

The Need That Drove Me To Desperation

From the time I was a little boy, I suffered with a tenacious dual character. In one respect, I possessed a nature so intense that I constantly lived on the fringes of excitability and even anger. My sharp personality intimidated some people and kept others at a distance. Resentment, pride, or selfishness sometimes sparked this harshness. Just as often, however, no premeditated malice was involved; the harshness simply came automatically. No matter how hard I tried to be different, my words always seemed to contain a certain undertone of sarcasm or hostility. I was extremely difficult to get along with. My unbearable nature usually invoked fear or outright anger in most people.

For all my brashness and "tough guy" facade, another side of my character was just as real. Inside I was deeply sensitive. I remember, as a child, feeling terribly vulnerable and fearful of the cutting remarks of my classmates, the abrasive comments of my father, and the foolish jokes of my friends. Outwardly, I had a tough exterior, but inwardly I wore a thin suit of skin. Of course, my touchy nature made me very defensive and overly protective.

To make matters worse, I grew up deeply insecure, living in a home characterized by strife. Oddly enough my personality was actually a perfect combination of those of my parents. My father was sharp-tongued and sarcastic. My mother was sensitive and insecure. Their incompatible union made for a miserable marriage, an unhappy home, and an unhealthy environment in which to raise a child. Like many other baby-boomers, being raised in an unloving home left me with a giant void. As a result, I constantly sought the acceptance of others in order to somehow fill this empty spot.

Combined, these factors opened a doorway to the dark, dismal world of sexual addiction which dominated my life for many years. From my earliest days I seemed to have had an inordinate attraction to sex in general and to women in particular. No longer content with girlie magazines or teenage conquests, my compulsive nature compelled me deeper and deeper into the world of perversion. What began as a perceived need for acceptance, which I thought could only be met in the throes of passion, gradually became an insatiable monster demanding increasingly more frequent and baser activity.

Although I could still function (albeit awkwardly) in social and work situations, my thinking became more and more bizarre. My deep-seated fear of people advanced until I was constantly plagued with paranoid thoughts. On one occasion, I was walking in a store when a young teenaged girl laughingly shoved her friend into me. Full of fear and embarrassment, I just knew they thought I was weird (and I was!). Immediately, I made a mad dash for home and sequestered myself in my mother's house for nearly a month.

Unfortunately, it was in this frame of mind and spirit that I lived most of my twenties. By the time I was 24, I had been through dozens of girlfriends and a wife. It was then that I met and married my wife, Kathy. Two anguish-filled years later, she ran off with another man and filed for divorce. At this point, I was finally ready to humble myself and admit my need for the Lord.

Becoming a Christian (and miraculously getting my wife back) dealt a real blow to the demons that had, up until this point, enjoyed great liberty tormenting and controlling me. It gave me a new purpose in life, an enthusiasm for something good and honorable. Becoming a believer did not instantly change my character. I was still Steve Gallagher. I still had a sharp tongue. I was still impatient. I still had thin skin. I was still socially awkward. And I was still very much bound up in sexual addiction.

Over the next three years I battled with the overwhelming temptations of lust. For most of my life I purposely went after thrilling experiences to escape the pain of life and in a futile attempt set out to gain a sense of self-worth as a man. Now, that worth was to be found in God alone. Becoming strong enough spiritually to put sexual sin down once and for all took a long time. Even though I battled with sexual temptation quite often, by God's grace I eventually found the freedom I needed.

Six months after my last encounter with another woman God led me to enter Bible school. Six months later He directed me to begin a ministry to help other men struggling with sexual sin. It began as a simple support group meeting in Sacramento once a week while I attended Bible school. The group's novelty caused word of it to spread. Before I knew it, I was appearing on national radio and television shows and preaching in various churches.

In 1989, Kathy and I bought a small farm in Kentucky and relocated the ministry there. At this time, we felt led by God to open it up as a live-in facility for men who needed more intensive help breaking free from the control of sexual addiction.

By the time men arrived at this new program in January 1990, I had been a Christian more than seven years. I soon discovered how little I acted like the One I claimed to represent and serve. It's one thing to appear on short media interviews or preach at churches where the people do not know you. Living with others in an environment where your uncrucified self can show its hideous face is completely different.

Regrettably, those men who came to me for help in those early years were probably sorely disappointed. Fortunately, people appreciated and respected my undeniable sincerity and intense zeal for God. It is also true that the Lord gave me clear insight concerning how to gain freedom from habitual sexual sin. However, I was still very full of myself. I was abrasive, prideful, and self-centered, and I was well aware of it. Romans seven best describes the constant helplessness and agony I experienced at seeing how unlike Christ I was. What particularly aggravated me was counseling men who were by nature warm, smooth, and friendly with others. They seemed so much more like Jesus than I was, despite the fact that I diligently sought after Him several hours each day. In contrast, however, their outward appearance of goodness was not matched by an enthusiasm about the things of God.

My constant failures, glaringly apparent to everybody around me, kept me crying out to God. Certainly, I was a different man. My tongue was more controlled than ever, but I was in a position where I could not afford to make mistakes. Each time I responded defensively or sarcastically, it exposed the selfish, prideful, and unloving nature still very much alive in me. Only Kathy knows my anguish over my constant failures during those early years of ministry.

To make matters even worse, I entered a time when my fellowship with God seemed to be drying up. Times of prayer had been the one place where I could get a temporary reprieve from my failures and feel as though I was accomplishing something for the Lord. They were a source of life and refreshment to me. But now when I prayed it seemed as though the heavens were brass. The Bible became stale and boring. My walk with God seemed lifeless.

I saw other Christians who seemed so happy, but I knew that for most of them it was simply a superficial happiness that was part of their character and always had been. And yet, though I felt I was doing everything right, I had no real joy or inner peace. Where was the bubbling fountain of life? Where was the abundant life promised to all believers in Christ? Where was my all-consuming love for God and others? Where was the joy of the Lord?

Just as I was about to lose all hope, God came into my dark, miserable world and started to open my eyes in a totally unexpected way. In November 1991, I visited a small, Pentecostal church where nobody knew me. The pastor preached hard from Luke six about what it means to be a Christian. "Love your enemies…Be merciful… Why do you call Me 'Lord, Lord,' and do not do what I say…?" The Lord hammered these words into my heart. I was bewildered about how I could be trying so hard to do right and yet be so far from God. When the pastor gave the altar call, I reluctantly trudged up the aisle—not because I felt compelled—but simply as one more emotionless, dry act of obedience. Convinced that I lacked the kind of love for God and others this man of God expressed in his sermon, I was willing to humble myself and ask for it.

At the altar, all the months (even years) of pent-up frustration came gushing out. My pride and selfishness became vividly real to me. I was broken over my lack of love for God and others. I drenched the altar with tears. In that brokenness came a fresh, new perspective I hadn't felt since my first-love days of 1982. Instantly, my intimacy with God was restored and a new compassion for the men at Pure Life bubbled up from within.

This giant leap forward for me was only the beginning. I needed more, much more. I had to learn how to live in this newfound life. I felt like a tiny baby crawling around the crib. I quickly realized that many of my perceptions about God and man were wrong, but what now? How could I correct my distorted ideas?

Shortly after this, in another one of those God-ordained events, I found out about a very special ministry located a couple hundred miles north of us. The Zion Faith Homes is a place where those in Christian service can go to find the Lord in a powerful way. A fellow minister told me, "The reason His voice can be heard more clearly there is primarily because of the deep level of consecration the ministers live in who run the place. If you are wanting to learn about living real Christianity, that's the place to go!" I asked one of my missionary friends if he had ever heard of the Faith Homes, and he told me in a hushed tone that it was a "powerhouse" where one could sense the Spirit of God in a dramatic way. Another pastor said that as soon as he walked through the front door he felt the Holy Ghost searching his heart, exposing sin, selfishness, pride, or questionable motives of his heart.

It sounded like the very thing I needed. Kathy and I didn't know what to expect the first time we visited. Would the people be super-spiritual weirdoes, out of touch with the realities of life? Or would they be in such close contact with God that they could read our thoughts? When we arrived at the Faith Homes that summer day of 1992, these and other questions filled our minds.

We were greatly relieved to find the people there—ministers, workers and trainees—to be the nicest, most normal folks we could have imagined. We did not get the sense that they were strange or cultic at all. In fact, as the days rolled by, we began to see their humility and unselfishness in a thousand different little ways. Despite my recent experience of brokenness, my selfishness and pride stood out in stark contrast to the way they demonstrated the love of Christ to other people.

We left a week later convinced that their relationship with the Lord was what we longed for. There was an abundance of life in their Christian experience that I had never seen before. I realized that I had witnessed the sort of Christianity Paul described throughout his writings. I was determined to have what they possessed.

Kathy and I began making two, three, and even four-week visits. When we visited, we took the role of trainees scrubbing dishes, floors, and toilets, and waiting on other guests. For the first time in our Christians lives, we learned what it really means to serve others.

God used my experience at the Faith Homes to humble me. As I diminished in my own estimation, a funny thing happened simultaneously: God became bigger! As I saw how unloving I was, I saw how full of love He is. As I saw how high-minded I was, I saw how humble He is. As I saw how selfish I was, I saw how unselfish He is. As I lost sight of my own supposed "goodness," I saw how good He is. Somehow, through it all, a true knowledge of God formed in my heart, changing the way I treated God and others.

Since that time, God has crushed me, humbled me, and disciplined me many times. Through it all, I have discovered who He is and what He is like. Perhaps even more importantly, He has reshaped my thinking and given me the heart transformation I so desperately needed. Although there are still faint traces occasionally observed by those close to me, for the most part, that sharp tongue, biting sarcasm, and hostile attitude have been swallowed up in a love which only my dear Lord could provide. God has surely met my deepest needs. I have discovered that His greatest work in my life has been at points of brokenness and helplessness when I realized my need for more of Him.

You might consider the way I have constantly turned to God

for help as a picture of defeat, not victory. However, it is my testimony that what God has done in my life will stand the test of time because it has been built upon the solid foundation of the Rock, not the shifting sands of human effort or emotion.

Meditation For Today

"No man, for any considerable period, can wear one face to himself and another to the multitude, without finally getting bewildered as to which may be the true."[1]
                          Nathaniel Hawthorne

"Solemn prayers, rapturous devotions, are but repeated hypocrisies unless the heart and mind be conformable to them."[2]
                          William Law

"There are only two kinds of men: the righteous who believe themselves sinners, and the rest, sinners who believe themselves righteous."[3]
                          Blaise Pascal

"I warn you that there is no connection whatsoever between the human manipulation of our emotions, on the one hand, and, on the other, the confirmation of God's revealed truth in our beings through the ministry of the Holy Spirit. When in our Christian experience our emotions are raised, it must be the result of what God's truth is doing for us. If that is not so, it is not properly religious stirring at all."[4]
                          A.W. Tozer

Chapter Two

Out Of The Clouds, Into Reality

One of the most disturbing experiences I have ever encountered in ministry happened in my Pure Life office a few years ago. I doubt if I will ever forget the look on Carl's face as he burst through my door and threw himself on the floor.

Carl was a very gifted singing evangelist. Over several years, he had developed a regular circuit of churches he ministered in throughout the South. Not only was he a talented singer, but he was also a charismatic preacher. He learned that people like "positive sermons," so he was always careful to leave congregations feeling good about themselves. People loved Carl's uplifting personality. No wonder pastors were happy to have him return year after year. For over 20 years he did just that, traveling from church to church, raising his family in a motor home.

At first, Carl was sincere. He originally entered the ministry out of a true desire to serve the Lord. As time went on, however, his dependence on God waned as he unconsciously relied on his own abilities. Carl learned how to look spiritual and impress congregations. People admired him and he knew it.

Eventually, he fell away from God. His Bible study ceased to be for his personal edification and became times to find sermon material. Having long since given up any kind of meaningful prayer life, a corruption took over inside that gradually manifested itself in his preaching. No longer willing to confront sin, Carl pandered a sugarcoated gospel. He considered himself an encourager, someone who makes you glad to be a Christian. In his mind, success was proof of God's blessing on his life.

Eventually, his weak spiritual condition caught up with him and he had a string of affairs with women in various churches. He came to Pure Life Ministries' live-in facility when his sin was exposed.

He was there only a few days when he had a life-defining moment out on the prayer trail behind the office. He was walking along when he suddenly had an encounter with God that left him devastated. What happened next will forever be etched in my mind.

Carl lay on the floor of my office screaming. The Lord had just revealed to him, in a way that only God can, that his 20 years of ministry had all been for himself. From the earliest days, he sought glory for himself, not God. He preached congregation-pleasing sermons, not what the Lord told him to preach. He went to places guaranteeing good offerings, not where the Lord directed him to go. In one instant of time, Carl saw that he had used his gifts and abilities for his own selfish gain. He realized that all of his work in ministry was empty and devoid of substance. In that moment, he saw a lifetime of service in the kingdom of God that had produced no fruit, no real results, and no eternal rewards. It was all for nothing. For one moment in a Kentucky hayfield, reality invaded Carl's make-believe, Pollyanna world. That sobering revelation was the only thing that saved him.

Spiritual Amateurs

Carl is the by-product of a system that has become strongly entrenched within the Church: a form of religion that resembles the real thing but is altered just enough to make it palatable for those unwilling to walk the narrow path of real Christianity. It peddles a counterfeit presentation of the gospel based on feelings rather than faith. This false version of Christianity is promoted by professional pitchmen who, like Carl, have become popular, not because of spiritual maturity, but because they instinctively know how to give people what they want.

Traveling evangelists aren't alone in propagating this emotionally based faith. Many pastors have built huge churches on the same kind of hype. Pastor Pete will serve as a good illustration of this type of minister. He leads a sprawling, big-city church full of ceaseless, bounding, jubilant activity. Such an atmosphere is a reflection of his own nature. Pete is, and has always been, positive, gregarious, fun loving, and uplifting to be around. When you attend one of his services nearly everything you hear will be positive: sermons about what God wants to do for you, testimonies about what God has done, and a worship service that resembles a Super Bowl victory party.

What's wrong with that? Am I against Christian enthusiasm? Absolutely not! I agree with those who ask the question, "Why do some believers get hysterical over a football game and yet refuse to show excitement over God?" I believe there is a place for genuine exuberance over our wonderful Savior and what He has done for us.

The problem with Pastor Pete's church is that when we peek behind the wall of outward exuberance and fluff, there is nothing there! The mature, discerning Christian sadly discovers that this church has no substance. The hope being peddled is not attached to a real knowledge of or dependence upon God, but rather upon a super-inflated climate of enthusiasm that is not allowed to dwindle. Consequently, this man's greatest fear is not that he could possibly be leading his flock astray, but rather that if he ever allowed the enthusiasm to die, all of his followers would quickly desert him for another church "where God is moving."

The Christian life is not meant to be lived continuously at a fever pitch. Being lost in the exhilaration of God's love or a mountaintop revelation of what He is like can be wonderfully encouraging in a believer's spiritual journey. Nevertheless, Christian growth usually comes from fighting through the thick foliage of life's problems down on the jungle floor, where true godly character is built and where the maturing believer learns what it means to live by faith in God.

Pastor Pete only has a superficial understanding of God, so it is all he can offer his congregation. In reality, he can shepherd them no further along the path than he has traveled in his own spiritual life. Since he has always been able to get by on his winsome personality, optimistic outlook, and energetic nature, he has never felt his need for anything deeper in God. Indeed, Pastor Pete learned early that his charismatic gifts made him a "natural-born leader," nullifying his need to cultivate the godly authority that comes from living in dependence on God. Simply put, Pastor Pete does not need God in order to attract followers.

Pastor Pete's quick smile and unceasing motion generates enthusiasm in others. A glance below the surface exposes some real problems in his ministry and in his personal life. The pseudo-mountain-top experiences he tries to produce for his followers are conceived out of his own wishful thinking. At some point in his walk with the Lord, Pete may have witnessed awesome manifestations of God's power in others. However, rather than seeking a genuine, personal experience with God, he is content to have a ministry full of zeal but lacking any real knowledge or spiritual weightiness. It is inevitable that every church service becomes a well choreographed, cheerleading event attempting to keep his congregation (i.e. spectators) electrified in an effort to maintain a high level of crowd-pleasing interest.

Instead of receiving the staples of a healthy spiritual diet, establishing the natural spiritual growth that occurs in a well-fed, maturely pastored congregation, church members receive a constant diet of cotton candy and marshmallow fluff, supplying a temporary burst of energy, but ultimately leaving them sorely malnourished. What else is expected from a man who has spent his entire Christian life omitting the primary elements of a well-balanced diet—the meat of being convicted by God's Word, the vegetables of discipline, the potatoes of sacrifice, the salad of adversity. He likes dessert and imagines that he and others can live on it all of the time. Thus, his church body resembles a drug addict who keeps himself going artificially while in reality starving his body of the proper nutrition needed to promote growth and sustain life.

Pastor Pete's lack of true, spiritual leadership shows not only in the pulpit, but also in his pastoral counseling. When approached by people needing real answers, Pastor Pete lends a sympathetic ear, gives a cheerful word of encouragement, says a fervent-sounding prayer, and ends with a reassuring slap on the back. Initially, the poor seeker feels uplifted for about 10 minutes before a bewildering sense of hopelessness sets in. Naturally, he has a difficult time understanding how such a word and prayer of encouragement could leave him feeling so confused and hopeless. What this hurting man needs is godly counsel from a pastor who has a sincere concern, truly understands his troubles, and prays with authority.

Unfortunately, a meeting with this pastor would disappoint just about anyone with a real need. Pete does not understand the various dilemmas of life many people face because he does not face his own. Compassion does not well up within him because he relies on sentiment and emotional responses to the pain of others. He offers no spiritual insight because he has never acquired the wisdom that comes to the person who has survived the dark night of the soul. He prays fervently but without power. His prayers are the emotional chatter of a frivolous man, not the God-moving, earnest pleas of an authentic intercessor. He talks about the life of victory, but his idea of what constitutes such a life is nothing but exaggerated statements that contain no spiritual reality. Consequently, the seeker leaves with no answers, no help, and no hope.

Pastor Pete has a very serious problem: his experience with God is extremely shallow. Thus, he remains superficial and immature, with nothing of substance to offer other people.

Faulty Foundation

Carl and Pete are spiritual amateurs who have no business being in positions of spiritual leadership. Since they lack personally meaningful relationships with God, they certainly cannot effectively represent Him to others in need. Moreover, their lack of true concern about other people deadens any possibility of real intercession at the throne of grace on behalf of those they are called to serve. Unfortunately, these two men typify the kind of spiritual leadership that is active in much of the Church.

Ostensibly, the message given by "hype peddlers" such as Carl and Pete is that people should put their faith in God. However, close examination of their teachings reveals that they are really instructing people to base their faith on the faulty foundation of a positive mental attitude rather than on the Rock of Ages. This skewed interpretation of Christianity produces temporary results for those whose mental outlook is buoyant by nature, but leaves the rest of Christendom feeling hopeless and defeated. These pseudo-ministers proclaim an unspoken message that victorious Christians are those who can regularly maintain their enthusiasm. They promote the idea that those who excel in the faith are the ones who can stimulate excitement in others.

The whole mess reminds me of the motivational meetings I was required to periodically attend as a real estate agent. First, leading sales associates offered testimonies of how they landed big contracts through persistent efforts. Next, a company leader gave the troops a stirring talk. The highlight of the get-together came when top salesmen were acknowledged for their efforts. The whole purpose of the meeting was to incite passion in the troops to sell more houses in the upcoming months.

The correlation between the two systems is remarkably similar. The "hype movement" (for lack of a better term) also has its testimonies of victory. Those who know how to inflame a crowd deliver stimulating sermons. Leading adherents to the movement are recognized as powerful men of God. It is easy to see why their methods are so successful at attracting followers. Instead of being humbled by a lack of godly characteristics, people are encouraged to see spirituality in the most optimistic light possible. Paul's warning that a person should not "...think more highly of himself than he ought to think; but to think so as to have sound judgment..." (Romans 12:3) fall on deaf ears because these followers are encouraged to carry an inflated view of personal piety. Meanwhile, any suggestion that they are exaggerating what they really have in Christ is often viewed as an attack from the devil.

Since these people think they are doing so well spiritually, they do not press into God, consecrate themselves, or deal seriously with the sin of the heart. Having been blinded by spiritual pride about the true condition of their souls, they do not see the need to do such things. They do not see their spiritual lack but see themselves as lacking nothing. In short, there is no need to be concerned about maturing in the faith because they are already at the top!

If Jesus addressed one of these power meetings today, perhaps He would say something along these lines: "Because you say, 'I am rich, and have become wealthy, and have need of nothing,' and you do not know that you are wretched and miserable and poor and blind and naked..." (Revelation 3:17) They do not see what they truly are because they are taught not to see.

Coming To God

Jesus once told a story about two men who went into the temple for the purpose of having an audience with God. The first, a religious leader, prayed: "God, I thank Thee that I am not like other people: swindlers, unjust, adulterers, or even like this tax-gatherer. I fast twice a week; I pay tithes of all that I get."

By today's outward standards, this man lived a godly life: praying, fasting, tithing, and abstaining from obvious, visible sin. He carefully gave God all the credit for the success he achieved. It is interesting to note that when he purveyed his life, everything he saw about himself was positive! I could see him easily fitting in with those who live in the realm of the hype movement.

The approach of the other man was quite different: "But the tax-gatherer, standing some distance away, was unwilling to lift up his eyes to heaven, but beat his breast, saying, 'God, be merciful to me, the sinner!'" This man did not march into the throne room of God and demand an audience. In fact, he stood off in the distance, unwilling even to look up at the Lord. Standing in the presence of the King, he was overwhelmed by his own unworthiness. His sins stood out glaringly in his mind as he bowed in the presence of the Holy One. He was sorrowful over his lack of Christ-likeness, ashamed at how little he had done for God. He stood there looking for one thing: mercy.

In today's upbeat church atmosphere, someone might suggest that this man needs to be reassured about "who he is in Christ," that he needs to accept God's love, and learn how to forgive himself. Some might even berate him for his negative attitude, labeling him as someone living a defeated life, a spiritual loser.

It's interesting how heaven's perspectives can be different from earth's. Jesus said, "I tell you, this man went down to his house justified rather than the other; for everyone who exalts himself shall be humbled, but he who humbles himself shall be exalted." (Luke 18:9-14)

The Proper Prognosis

The issue is not so much the way a person prays but whether

or not he truly has a clear understanding of his own need. If he sees himself in the proper light, he approaches God with a humble spirit. On the other hand, if he pumps himself up to be something that he isn't, he will attempt to storm heaven in spiritual arrogance and presumption. The way a person prays flows out of the way he views himself in relation to the Lord.

Prideful people prefer to see themselves in a positive light. Matthew nine provides a fitting example. Jesus was sitting in the home of Matthew the tax collector, surrounded by those considered to be "low-lifes." As is so often the case today, it is the down-and-outers, the troubled, those given over to outward sin who see their need for His help. The religious leaders standing outside did not feel that same sense of urgency. Like the Pharisee praying in the temple, they were fully confident of their spiritual condition. Nevertheless, Jesus came outside and made one of the most poignant statements found in Scripture: "It is not those who are healthy who need a physician, but those who are sick...I did not come to call the [self] righteous, but sinners." This statement describes one of the most important characteristics of those who truly walk in victory: their spiritual need keeps them in close proximity to the One who can meet that need.

Some Christians believe that salvation ends the desperate need for God's involvement in their lives. Now, they can move forward in their journey toward heaven. In reality, maturing believers grow in awareness of the need for God's constant involvement. Instead of leaving the Lord back at the starting gate, they see Him at the finish line. Realizing the necessity for His help, guidance, correction, and discipline to live victoriously keeps them constantly turning to the Lord.

By contrast, the shallow believer who is not willing to pay the price of pursuing God prefers to invent a godliness of his own imagination. He might try to impress others with what a seeker he is, but the reality of his life with God is that he is quite content to settle for the fake. He is not spiritually healthy; he refuses to acknowledge his sick condition because he is not willing to follow the prescribed treatment needed to correct it. It is much easier to contrive an exaggerated sense of spiritual well-being than to fight for the real thing.

Jesus spoke of a group of people who suffered from this same kind of self-deception. They too imagined that they were walking with God. Judgment Day's reality exposed something different. "Not everyone who says to Me, 'Lord, Lord,' will enter the kingdom of heaven; but he who does the will of My Father who is in heaven," Jesus said. "Many will say to Me on that day, 'Lord, Lord, did we not prophesy in Your name, and in Your name cast out demons, and in Your name perform many miracles?' And then I will declare to them, 'I never knew you; depart from Me, you who practice lawlessness'" (Matthew 7:21-23).

Notice that these people were doing all the right things outwardly: identifying themselves with the name of the Lord, prophesying, casting out demons, and even performing miracles. It shows that a person can have wonderful works, even to the point of somehow tapping into the power of God, and yet still be in terrible trouble. Unlike the evangelist who came into our live-in program, these people did not face reality until it was too late.

The fact of the matter is that until a man comes to grip with his desperate condition before God, he will never be broken, never have a real repentance, and never enjoy the abundance made available to the child of God. Instead, he can fully expect his lot to be one of defeat, emptiness, and a false sense of victory that is based on nothing but hype.

Meditation For Today

"You've got to deceive yourself before you can be deceived."

                Anonymous

"A wise man will be master of his mind, a fool will be its slave."

                Publius Syrus

"God is not concerned about our happiness but about our holiness."[1]

                Leonard Ravenhill

"You must be brought to the conviction that your life is a guilty and shameful life... It must become a matter of earnest resolve with you that your life is to undergo a complete transformation."[2]

                Andrew Murray

Chapter Three

A World At War

King Eshly was quite insane. Weak-willed and controlled by his passions, he indulged in numerous vices on a regular basis. Mercifully, his country was tiny, making his sphere of influence insignificant. In fact, the nation's only claim to fame was that it bordered the territory of a regional super-power whose king was known far and wide for his benevolence and kindness. King Sus was adored by his people and respected by his enemies. In his madness, Eshly often forgot how fortunate he was to border such a kingdom.

The contrast between the two kingdoms stood out glaringly. The nation Sus reigned over was well managed, clean, and orderly. Eshley's country showed all of the signs of a poorly run state.

Not often, but every now and then, Eshley enjoyed periods of sanity, during which he was prone to make prudent decisions. Knowing this, Tellius, Eshley's chief counselor, waited for the right opportunity to approach the king with a radical proposal. Believing his plan was just what their hapless country needed, Tellius waited patiently for the next moment of sanity to appear.

Finally, the day arrived. Tellius immediately recognized the look of sensibility on the king's face. "King Eshly, may I have a word with you?"

"Of course, Tellius," Eshly replied. "Speak your mind and don't hold back. I feel pretty good today."

"King Eshly, the country is in great disrepair. Our government is full of corruption. The municipal department is in shambles. The army is so discouraged we experience small insurrections almost weekly. In short, Eshly, the country is in grave trouble. If something isn't done about it immediately, there may never be any hope for restoration."

"What are we to do, Tellius? Tell me what to do!"

"When other kingdoms faced similar crises, they invited Sus to take over their kingdoms. King Sus's ability to govern allows these nations to experience tremendous results!"

"I know this is right, Tellius. Send word to Sus right away. I want him to come in."

That week, the army of Sus entered the tiny country and established a base of operations just inside the border. Meanwhile, Eshly reverted back to his insanity. Compounding the problem, Eshly's evil counselor, Terlock, heard of the decision. "Oh great King Eshly, what have you done? Sus has invaded our beloved country! Don't you realize he will take away everything dear to us? He will put a stop to your parties, take away your concubines, and ruin all your fun; he will make you rule the country his way. You will lose control. Oh King, give me the order and our armies will attack immediately, driving him out of the country!"

Eshly was confused. What Tellius had told him seemed so sensible at the time, but he also knew Terlock was right. Sus *would* change everything. On the other hand, having Sus in your kingdom had its advantages. Nations attached to Sus were prosperous and secure. "Here are my orders, Terlock. I don't want you to attack Sus. We can gain much from him. Therefore, we will allow him to stay in the country, but only on our terms. We will simply resist any changes we don't agree with. Besides, everybody knows what a sap he is. He won't do anything about it!"

It seemed to Eshly that he could enjoy the best of both worlds. An alliance with Sus would provide prosperity and security, but Eshly could stay in control of his own kingdom. The reality of the situation, however, was that the kingdom remained in disrepair. The problems continued that plagued it for so long. While there was a change in outward allegiance, life went on much the same as before.

By now, I am certain you have realized that this fable is an illustration of the Lord invading a person's "inside world" and describes a battle that constantly rages within believers: fl-Eshly versus Je-Sus. As goes a person's level of sanity, so goes the war.

The Enemy of God

Very few Christians realize how much they resist God. The truth is, we are all like King Eshly: existing most of the time in the insanity of fallen, human thinking (There is a way which seemeth right unto a man...). During our occasional lapses of sanity, the Spirit of God is able to communicate to us. We have allowed Jesus in, but we keep His authority at bay. Why? Because we do not want Him telling us how to live our lives. We are content to obey outwardly and superficially but not from the heart.

We all face the struggle of dealing with our flesh. Paul said, "For the mind set on the flesh is death, but the mind set on the Spirit is life and peace, because the mind set on the flesh is hostile toward God..." (Romans 8:6-7). Imagine it! Hostile to God!

There is a part of us which loves Him. Our spirit has been awakened, and we have taken baby steps toward loving Him as He commands. Yet, of the 50,000 thoughts we entertain in any given day, how many revolve around Him? How many are centered on meeting the needs of those whom He loves? The bulk of our thinking revolves around ourselves: what we want, what we like, what we are interested in, and what we want to do. This kind of thinking is what is at odds with the kingdom of God. In fact, our thinking is utter selfishness, completely foreign to God's kingdom.

Living in victory requires a drastic change in this kind of thinking. Getting a selfish, worldly human to think like Christ is no small undertaking and partially explains why so few ever reach real victory. God's first challenge in this feat is helping the person see the error of his thinking. Unfortunately, we are like a man in a psychiatric ward who has lost touch with reality and yet thinks he is normal because those around him are so crazy! If he ever hopes to be released from that place, he will have to acknowledge the fact that he does not think soundly. From there, a good counselor (such as Tellius) can guide him into proper thinking. Anybody in the field of counseling knows that until a person admits he has a problem with the way he thinks, there is absolutely nothing that can be done to help him.

To further exacerbate the problem, the person God is working on often resists His efforts. It is like a technician called in to fix a malfunctioning computer. The central processing unit that is putting out bad data and making faulty calculations is the same unit that must cooperate with the technician's efforts to fix it. When the technician tries to fix the CPU, he finds that it counters his every move inside. There is something in its faulty circuitry (pride) that denies there is anything wrong and attempts to stop his efforts. When the technician attempts to introduce accurate data that will induce the hard drive to correct the fault, the computer rejects the information.

Many believers fight tooth and nail against the One trying to help them! They resist Him. They ignore Him. They disobey Him. They pay attention when it is convenient and disregard Him the rest of the time. Why are people so hostile to our wise and loving Father? Life would be so much better if we allowed Sus to run our country, yet the insanity that makes us do such a lousy job is the very thing that keeps telling us that we are better off without His rule.

God's greatest challenge in bringing His people into victorious living is to make them realize their need for His control in their lives. This is an extremely delicate operation, requiring an enormous amount of effort on His part. Nevertheless, the Lord graciously overlooks our faults, patiently awaits His opportunities to reason with us, and accomplishes as much as He can with the little He has to work with. While the Lord is a gentleman and refuses to use force to accomplish His goals, make no mistake about it, He has one thing in mind: the absolute conquest of our "inside world."

Before we can fully grasp the challenge of this process we must gain a better understanding of the flesh.

The Weak Willed Man

Jesus possessed a godly self-composure when He walked this earth. When people needed a sympathetic ear, a shoulder to cry on, or the strength to bear their burdens, they looked to Him. However, there came a night when Jesus, overwhelmed with His own problems, asked for help. That night He turned to His three closest friends and asked them to pray Him through His ordeal. He only asked for their help one time, yet they failed Him. "The spirit is willing, but the flesh is weak," He sighed. Those nine words describe the battle that all believers must face in life.

We all have a flesh and it does not magically vanish when a person becomes a believer. The flesh is our old, carnal nature. It must be dealt with. Think of it as the weak-willed man within us. Like King Eshly, our fallen nature has a side to it that has no character, no resolve, no backbone, and no self-control.

The Bible says that the flesh is a slave to impurity and lasciviousness (Romans 6:19), serves the law of sin (Romans 7:25), has passions and desires (Galatians 5:24), brings corruption (Galatians 6:8), has its own wisdom (II Corinthians 1:12), wages war against the soul (I Peter 2:11) and has nothing good in it (Romans 7:18). It is the flesh that desires and generates immorality, impurity, sensuality, idolatry, sorcery, enmities, strife, jealousy, outbursts of anger, disputes, dissensions, factions, envying, drunkenness, and carousing. (Galatians 5:19-21) It is the weak-willed man inside us.

When we speak of the flesh, or the carnal nature, keep in mind that we are primarily referring to a mind-set, a way of thinking. It is the insanity which keeps us bound up in sin that we know (when we are in our right minds) is destroying us.

For the man struggling with the powerful pull of sexual temptation, the conflict between the flesh and spirit becomes an even more relevant issue in life. Paul said, "This I say then, walk in the Spirit, and ye shall not fulfill the lust of the flesh." (Galatians 5:16 KJV)

Herein is the key to overcoming life-dominating habits: to walk in the Spirit. After 15 years of dealing with Christian men in sexual sin (including many ministers), I have never found any evidence to dispute this statement. Childhood traumas, frigid wives, availability of pornography, seductive women, or lack of accountability notwithstanding, I have never seen a man in sexual sin who was walking in the Spirit. Every man I have ever dealt with has had one thing in common: not one of them emphasized the need to crucify the flesh (as Paul later mentions in the passage) and to walk in the Spirit.

You can spend years on the psychologist's couch, regularly

attend support group meetings, go to a world famous clinic for sexual addicts, have experiences of a memory being healed, be slain in the Spirit, or even have demons cast out of you. However, if you want to overcome habitual sin, you must learn to walk in the Spirit.

In Chapter One, I described how God had "crushed me, humbled me, and disciplined me many times." Perhaps this sounds as though I feel God has been unmerciful to me; but actually it was all mercy. Solomon once said, "Like a city that is broken into and without walls is a man who has no control over his spirit" (Proverbs 25:28). I lacked the mental control that comes from a character formed by Christ. As a result, my mind and will were being over-run by the enemy. It was my Heavenly Father's discipline that brought my wild mind under subjection to the Holy Spirit.

This process is a lifelong daily battle. After telling his readers to walk in the Spirit, Paul goes on to say, "For the flesh sets its desire against the Spirit, and the Spirit against the flesh; for these are in opposition to one another, so that you may not do the things that you please" (Galatians 5:17). In this verse, we see the daily battle raging inside every believer who wants to please God and yet finds that part of him simply wants to indulge in pleasure and sin.

Everyday we make choices about which spirit will be in control. We can choose to give in to the flesh: vent our anger on others, be sarcastic, indulge in sexual thinking, and be wrapped up in ourselves. We can sit in front of a television, listen to carnal music, or read worldly magazines. Or, we can choose to shield ourselves from the sensualities of the media, control our minds, bridle our tongues, and show kindness to others. Minute by minute, throughout the rest of our lives, we will face choices as to our behavior.

This is where the typical Christian gets bogged down and discouraged. It seems that change will never come, that they are bound to live in defeat. This is not God's desire for His children. While it is true that one aspect of the spirit vs. flesh war occurs in our daily lives, equally true is that the person who strives after righteousness, struggles against the desires of the flesh, and pursues a course of holiness, gradually gains ground in the contest. This process takes time and requires the believer to diligently cooperate with the Holy Spirit's work. The sincere seeker soon discovers a previously unknown strength forming within him. He will notice that temptations no longer grip him with overwhelming power. His intimacy with God increases, in turn producing a power not present early on in his faith to overcome temptation. Before long, this man will come to know what it means to become a mature saint: to truly walk in the Spirit.

This spiritual growth and development is not automatic. A person does not mature into godliness simply because his salvation experience happened a long time ago. He grows into the likeness of Christ only by daily cooperating with God's work in his inner man.

One of the first things he must learn is bringing his flesh under subjection. Many sexual addicts plead with God for help to overcome sexual addiction but resist Him when He begins to require change in other areas of their lives. They want Him to come into their inside world and clean out the red light district but leave the movie houses, gambling halls, and comedy clubs.

When men come into the Pure Life live-in program, they quickly find out that God is not looking to simply help them overcome "one little problem." Rather, He is looking to overhaul their entire lives. These men's lives can be compared to an old, dilapidated shack. God wants to dismantle the old dump and build a palace, but many shriek in terror when they see Him show up with the hammer and crow bar. They feel like they will die if He takes it down. Instead of allowing the Lord to destroy it, they go out and nail a few boards on it, give it a fresh coat of paint and try to convince Him that it is now a worthy dwelling. There's nothing more pathetic than a well-painted shack! This is precisely what Jesus was referring to when He said, "And no one puts new wine into old wineskins; otherwise the wine will burst the skins, and the wine is lost, and the skins as well; but one puts new wine into fresh wineskins" (Mark 2:22). How can the Lord get us out of the slums of defeat if we refuse to allow Him?

God wants to give us something extremely precious: the mind of His Son Jesus. Why do we resist Him, insisting that we keep our old, carnal, insane way of thinking? A person will never overcome sexual sin by focusing on overcoming sexual sin. He will only overcome sexual sin as he allows God to revamp his entire carnal nature by reproducing the nature of Christ within him. Everything that keeps him from walking in the Spirit must go. Paul describes this process of mortifying the flesh and being filled with the Spirit:

> Put to death, therefore, whatever belongs to your earthly nature: sexual immorality, impurity, lust, evil desires and greed, which is idolatry. Because of these, the wrath of God is coming. You used to walk in these ways, in the life you once lived. But now you must rid yourselves of all such things as these: anger, rage, malice, slander, and filthy language from your lips. Do not lie to each other, since you have taken off your old self with its practices and have put on the new self, which is being renewed in knowledge in the image of its Creator... Therefore, as God's chosen people, holy and dearly loved, clothe yourselves with compassion, kindness, humility, gentleness and patience. Bear with each other and forgive whatever grievances you may have against one another. Forgive as the Lord forgave you. And over all these virtues put on love, which binds them all together in perfect unity (Colossians 3:5-14 NIV).

These words are a clear map to follow, a laid-out course: the path to the life of Christian maturity. As we rid ourselves of the old nature, God replaces the void with the mind, thinking, and behavior of Christ. Figuratively speaking, as we allow Sus to have more of the territory in our kingdom, we will find that our inside world becomes better managed and more clean and orderly. As we permit God to empty our old self-nature, we find Him filling us with His Holy Spirit. Thus, a defeated life is gradually replaced with a victorious life.

The Lifelong War

The graph found in graph 3-1 (following page) is what the spiritual growth of a carnal Christian looks like. You will notice the ups and downs of life which we all face. The up-swings represent those times when things go well spiritually. The downturns illustrate periods of struggle: storms that beat against both the house of the

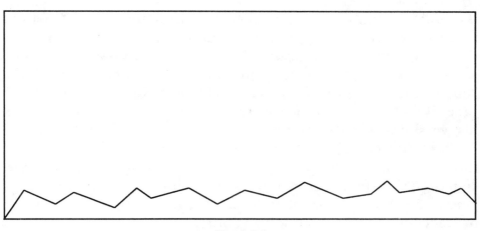

Graph 3-1

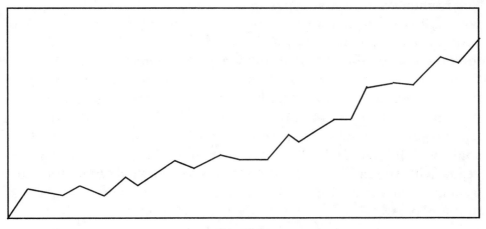

Graph 3-2

wise and of the fool. (Matthew 7) Take note that this person experiences no sustained spiritual growth. After years of going to church, he is essentially in the same place spiritually as when he began. He has not learned from his failures or taken the necessary steps to grow.

In graph 3-2 (above) we see the same ups and downs in life. This man has times when he feels spiritually dry, when he cannot sense the presence of God. He faces failures and must deal with times of discouragement. He even has times of apathy. In every respect, he faces the same storms as the carnal Christian shown in graph 3-1. Notice, however, that the general flow of his spiritual life is upward. Unlike the stagnant, unhealthy life of the carnal Christian, which never seems to get any better, the maturing believer continues to grow through all of his struggles. You will also notice that after a while, he actually gets to the place in his spiritual life where his "down" times of spiritual dryness are higher than his previous "up" times. In other words, he has matured in the Lord to the point where his worst day is better than his best day was previously.

The process of maturing in the faith is a recurrent theme throughout the entire New Testament. We repeatedly read that the sign of new birth is a growth in spiritual graces. In fact, Paul even goes so far as to say that this is the purpose for the different positions of leadership within the Body of Christ. (Ephesians 4:11-13)

God expects growth from His children. Growth is what allowed Peter when writing his letters to the church to be so full of grace, while 30 years earlier he was constantly shooting off his mouth and acting carnally. This is why Thomas became so full of faith that he took the gospel all the way to India and died a martyr's death, even though earlier he had doubted the Lord's resurrection. This is why toward the end of John's life, he was able to receive something as tremendous as the Revelation, even though 60 years earlier he had tried to get the Lord to call fire down from heaven upon some hapless souls who did not respond the way he thought they should. For 2,000 years the testimony of the Church has been established and maintained by saints who have allowed God to do His glorious, sanctifying work in their lives.

Much more than most of us realize, we need God's work in our lives. It is not overstating it to say that we desperately need Him to spiritually invade and take over our inside world. As God captures our hearts, conquers our wills, and fills us with His Spirit, we will experience the victorious life we are promised. This is what the Lord desires for us and expects from us.

Meditation For Today

"We have learned to live with unholiness and have come to look upon it as the natural and expected thing."[1]
A.W. Tozer

"Many professing Christians are pleased if their minister adopts a low standard and is ready to hope that almost everybody is a Christian. It is easy to see why they are pleased with such an exhibition of Christianity—it serves their main design and helps them maintain what they call a 'comfortable hope,' although they do so little for God."[2]
Charles Finney

"Man's chief care, his highest virtue, and his only happiness, now and through all eternity, is to present himself as an empty vessel in which God can dwell and manifest His power and goodness."[3]
Andrew Murray

"People imagine that dying to self makes one miserable. But it is just the opposite. It is the refusal to die to self that makes one miserable. The more we know of death with Him, the more we shall know of His life in us, and so the more of real peace and joy."[4]
Roy Hession

Chapter Four

God Is Not Satisfied

Roger is a Christian attorney who resides in California. A man of success, Roger is continually sought out for prominent positions within his church and has served on the boards of several ministries. Spiritual maturity did not seem to be an issue of concern when his services were sought.

Certainly, Roger is a competent attorney, but his demanding attitude, arrogant demeanor, and quick temper make him nearly impossible to work with. To further exasperate his co-workers, he is unwilling to accept responsibility for his actions. When he does something wrong he justifies himself or simply blames someone else. Since he never learns from his mistakes, he never changes.

Unfortunately, the ministers who were in a position to help him over the years did not dare approach him about his ungodly behavior. They were using him for his legal expertise and were careful not to offend him. Because of their selfish motives, he was allowed to live in delusion about his spiritual life.

Tragically, Roger's story is fairly typical in today's Church. By and large, we no longer demand holiness from our ministers, consecration from our teachers, or Christian maturity from our deacons. Apparently, charisma, worldly success, and influence have replaced godly character as the important characteristics of leadership. In short, the Church in America is content with shallow Christianity. We could have so much more if we could only see our need for it!

With this understanding in mind, the graph on the following page loosely illustrates three different plateaus of the Christian journey. Life, of course, is never as cut and dry as this graph, and yet I think it will help map out the course God looks for us to take in life.

When a person comes to the Lord, he begins at the starting line, ground zero, as it were. Up to this point, he has only known self-rule, self-determination, and self-pleasing. Now suddenly, a new King is there, along with a new direction in life. From the beginning, the Lord reveals His love and grace. He also makes it clear that He is looking for on-going change to take place in the person's life.

While the Lord has a wonderful strategy to accomplish this great work, it requires the new believer's cooperation. Each of us faces the same choices and the same paths. If God had His way, every believer would become a Peter, Thomas, or John. Our God isn't a capricious Master who holds favorites. He desires all believers to walk in godliness and holiness.

If a person has experienced real repentance and is sincere in his desire to mature, it does not take long for him to arrive at the first plateau depicted on the graph. Outward obedience, faithfulness in daily devotions, freedom from habitual sin, and the budding of the fruit of the Spirit now characterize this believer's daily life.

While it is wonderful to arrive at the first plateau, the true seeker determined to find God will not be content to remain there. He presses on to the second plateau. Those who attain this level are not merely outwardly obedient, but are obedient in the heart as well. Their relationships with God grow deeper as He is allowed to conquer their natures. Whether or not these folks are in official ministry positions, there is no question that they have a genuine love for the Lord.

Beyond this plateau is a third level into which few venture. This is a place where the saint has entered into a profound intimacy with the Lord that comes from a deep consecration. He is lost in a love for his Savior characterized in part by the complete absence of any self will. He has such a poverty of spirit that the daily reality of his life is his great need for God. That sense of urgency keeps him

Plateaus of the Christian Journey

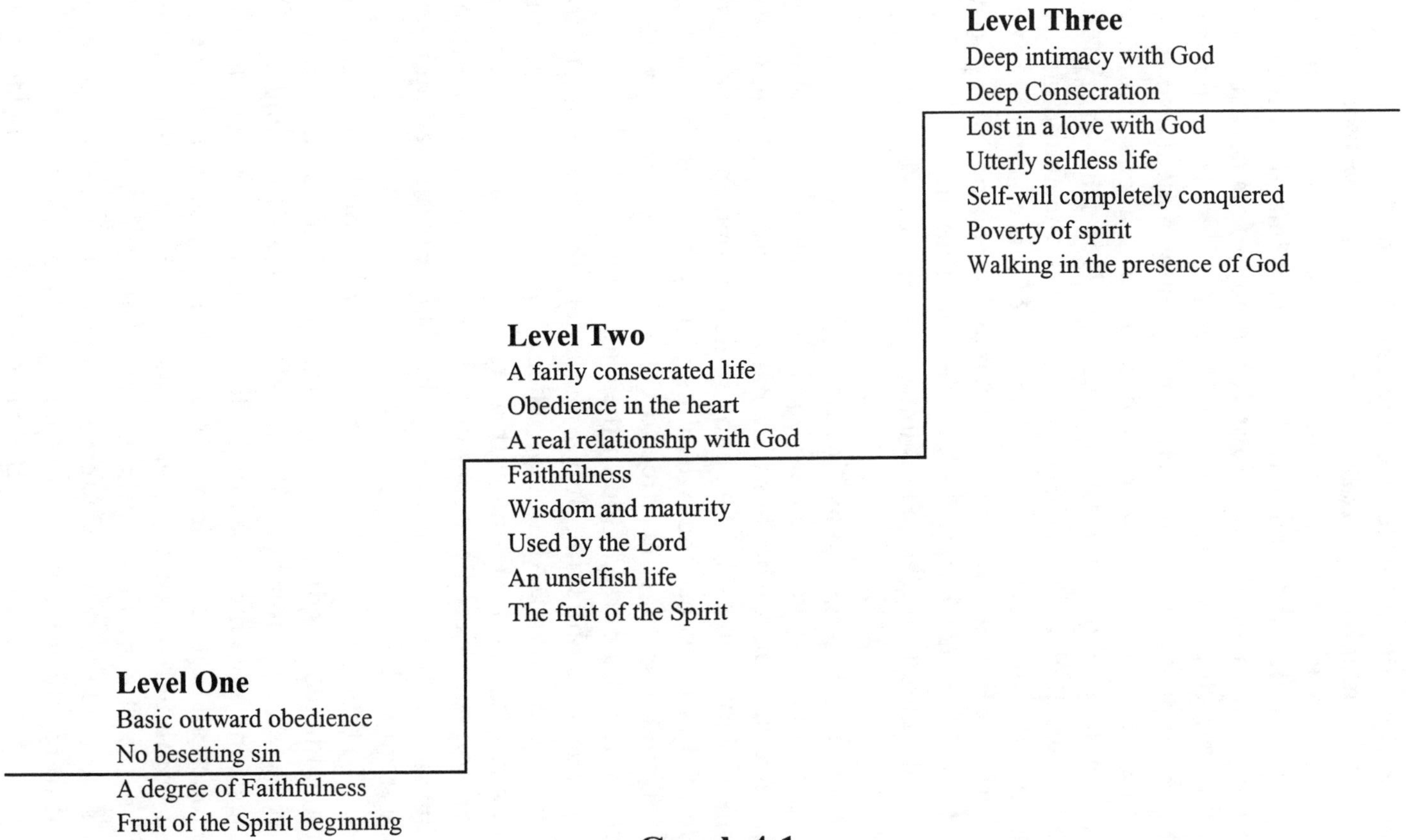

Level Three

Deep intimacy with God
Deep Consecration

Lost in a love with God
Utterly selfless life
Self-will completely conquered
Poverty of spirit
Walking in the presence of God

Level Two

A fairly consecrated life
Obedience in the heart
A real relationship with God

Faithfulness
Wisdom and maturity
Used by the Lord
An unselfish life
The fruit of the Spirit

Level One

Basic outward obedience
No besetting sin

A degree of Faithfulness
Fruit of the Spirit beginning

Graph 4-1

continually walking in the presence of the Lord.

This graph helps the reader establish how lofty his goals should be in his pursuit of God. The Lord is not satisfied with lukewarm living and mediocre commitment but longs for a deeper intimacy with His people. However, many of us forget about the holiness of God. We lose sight of the fact that He expects every believer to press in to know Him in a greater way and to love Him more deeply. This was true in the lives of biblical characters. It is no different today. God is not satisfied because He wishes every follower to penetrate the closer regions, to experience the abundant life, and to know Him in a very real way. The title of this chapter is not meant to represent Him as an impatient, demanding despot who can never be pleased, but as a loving Father who yearns to mature His children in the intimate knowledge and understanding of who He is.

When Being Upright Was Not Enough

In the first verse of the book that goes by his name, Job is described as a man who "was blameless, upright, fearing God, and turning away from evil." The book indicates that Job lived in such a state of righteousness that when his sons were together for a feast, Job offered a special sacrifice to God, thinking "perhaps my sons have sinned and cursed God in their hearts."

After establishing Job's character, the scene shifts to the throne room of the Almighty, where Satan is seen slithering in among the angels. Beaming with a certain parental pride, God asks, "Have you considered My servant Job? For there is no one like him on the earth, a blameless and upright man, fearing God and turning away from evil."

To this the devil rasps, "Does Job fear God for nothing? Hast Thou not made a hedge about him and his house and all that he has, on every side? Thou hast blessed the work of his hands, and his possessions have increased in the land. But put forth Thy hand now and touch all that he has; he will surely curse Thee to Thy face." God must continually face the devil's sneering accusation that people only serve Him if they selfishly get something out of it. Without Job's knowledge, a dare uttered in an entirely different realm is about to result in his whole life being turned upside-down.

We know the story. A Sabean cattle-rustling ring stole all his herds, a mysterious fire destroyed several thousand sheep, and an aberrant tornado decimated his family. All of this in one day! And if that were not enough, suddenly Job finds himself covered with angry, red boils. Job responded to all this worshipping God and saying, "Naked I came from my mother's womb, and naked I shall return there. The LORD gave and the LORD has taken away. Blessed be the name of the LORD." Through all of these difficult situations, Job did not sin or blame God. Truly Job was a man who was upright before the Lord. Yet, God allowed all of this to happen because He wanted Job's spiritual life to experience something deeper.

For the next 40 chapters of the book, perhaps covering many months of spiritual uncertainty, Job continues in his ordeal. Some of his well-intentioned friends show up and give their opinions. Job spouts off his impressions of the circumstances as well.

Suddenly, out of nowhere, the Almighty arrives, confronting Job about spiritual pride. "Who is this that darkens counsel by words without knowledge? Now gird up your loins like a man, and I will ask you, and you instruct Me! Where were you when I laid the foundation of the earth? Tell Me, if you have understanding, who set its measurements, since you know? Or who stretched the line on it?" The thundering sermon continued, leaving Job shaking and cringing. "Behold, I am insignificant;" the humbled man finally replies. "What can I reply to Thee?"

God was still not satisfied with the achieved result. It was a beginning. Job had been taken down "the ladder" a few notches, but the Lord was looking for a more complete humbling. So for two more chapters He continues to boom out His oration. Finally, the storm of God's thundering voice having ceased, Job squeaks out his reply, "I have heard of Thee by the hearing of the ear; but now my eye sees Thee; therefore I retract, and I repent in dust and ashes."

This is what God wanted to accomplish in the life of Job. Yes, Job was an upright man, but it is obvious by the things he expressed to his friends that he had become a little too confident in his own righteousness. The Lord was not satisfied with his spiritual level and allowed him to undergo one of the greatest divine crucibles ever recorded in the history of God's dealings with man.

Most people flinch at stories like this. Greatly relieved that Job's fortune was restored at the end of the story, they miss the entire point of everything the poor man endured. The Lord was doing a great work in his life. Yes, Job enjoyed his riches for a few more decades, but what God accomplished *inside* him he has enjoyed for thousands of years!

When An Outstanding Faith Was Not Enough

We can also study a young man of about 20 years. By this time in David's life, Samuel had secretly anointed him king. David had killed a bear and a hungry lion. He was a national hero for defeating a nine-foot giant with a slingshot and bringing about the death of thousands of Philistines. Things could not have looked more promising for this 20-year-old Israelite, and yet God was not satisfied. He wanted David to have a deeper spiritual experience before he sat on Israel's throne.

In Chapter 18 of 1 Samuel, we learn what happened when the Lord began to allow things to unravel in David's life. "Now it came about on the next day that an evil spirit from God came mightily upon Saul, and he raved in the midst of the house, while David was playing the harp with his hand, as usual; and a spear was in Saul's hand. And Saul hurled the spear for he thought, 'I will pin David to the wall.' But David escaped from his presence twice."

Just when everything looked so promising for young David, God orchestrated a series of events that caused David to flee for his life. For the next 13 years, he and his men lived in the wilderness, separated from their loved ones, hiding from Saul.

Most people of Israel wanted to see David immediately established as king. Think of the heartache they could have been spared had Saul been removed from the throne. He was a terrible king, ruling the country as a cruel dictator. It would have been so easy for God to remove Saul from the picture so that David could have his rightful place on the throne. But no, God allowed this ungodly, degenerate man to run the country right into the ground. Why? Because what He planned to accomplish in the inner life of this young man was even more important to Him than the smooth running of His entire kingdom on earth.

The fact that God dealt with His anointed this way is very difficult for many modern Christians to accept, especially those who emphasize the outward signs of success in ministry rather than the character of the man who runs it. The Lord is not awed with the size of a ministry's budget. The number of radio stations a preacher is heard on does not impress Him, or even how many people are supposedly being "saved." God is interested in people entering into a love relationship with Him. He is concerned about the cultivation of true disciples. He is looking for men who know what it means to walk with God. The work that God accomplishes within a person's heart means everything to Him.

To the sincere believers alive during David's time, it must have seemed like such a disaster when he was run out of the country. For the following 13 years, the people of Israel were forced to languish under the tyrannical rule of a devil-possessed madman. However, the Lord did a great work in David's life during that time. What was accomplished inside David during those extremely difficult years allowed him to build Israel into a mighty nation. For 3,000 years since then, believers sincerely striving to develop an intimacy with God find much-needed help in the Psalms; profound spiritual words from David as a result of what God accomplished within him.

The Lord's ways are not our ways. Achieving great exploits for the kingdom of God has its place, but a person's personal battles are what yield eternal results.

When Remarkable Revelations Were Not Enough

The last person's life we will examine is the Apostle Paul. Before his salvation, Paul established himself as one of the most promising young religious leaders in the Pharisee sect. His introduction to Christianity was nothing less than a vision of Jesus on the Damascus road. After a number of years of preparation, God used him to establish churches all over the regions of Galatia, Pisidia, and Asia. God also used this one man to establish a beachhead for the gospel in the dark continent of Europe. By the time Paul wrote his second epistle to the Corinthians, he had enjoyed enormous success in ministry and knew an extensive array of spiritual experiences, including being taken up into the third heaven. Despite this success, the Lord was not satisfied. Paul tells what happened at this point in his life:

> "And because of the surpassing greatness of the revelations, for this reason, to keep me from exalting

myself, there was given me a thorn in the flesh, a messenger of Satan to buffet me—to keep me from exalting myself! Concerning this I entreated the Lord three times that it might depart from me. And He has said to me, 'My grace is sufficient for you, for power is perfected in weakness.' Most gladly, therefore, I will rather boast about my weaknesses, that the power of Christ may dwell in me. Therefore I am well content with weaknesses, with insults, with distresses, with persecutions, with difficulties, for Christ's sake; for when I am weak, then I am strong." (II Corinthians 12:7-10)

According to Scripture, the Lord sent a troubling demon to afflict Paul, to keep him out of spiritual pride. Paul was turning the whole world upside-down for Jesus Christ. Who cares about a little pride? Apparently, God does. Paul was a prize possession and God was not willing to lose the closeness the two of them enjoyed for the sake of ministerial success. This story is a picture of God's holy jealousy over the love of a devoted follower's life. He knew only too well that if Paul began rising up in pride that he would drift away, lose his spiritual effectiveness, and perhaps even bring dishonor to the kingdom of heaven. So God gave Paul the gift of a thorn in the flesh: a harassing, oppressing spirit to keep him humbled.

Before going any further with our subject, it is worth noting that the devil played a role in forming the characters of all three of these men. Those with a worldly, success-is-everything perspective cannot fathom such a thing. However, we are facing the fact that the Lord is more concerned with the believer's spiritual life than with the success of his personal ministry.

There is something about unchecked success that fosters self-reliance, self-sufficiency, and eventually, self-glory. Left on our own, we inescapably become strong in ourselves. Before you know it, the success of our Christian service becomes more important to us than the Lord himself.

God does not need men with powerful personalities. He needs weak ones who know how to depend on Him. The Almighty does not need vessels full of themselves and their own talents. He needs empty vessels that can be filled with His power. The Lord does not need ministers with tremendous preaching competence. He needs men of meekness whose tongues are controlled by the Holy Spirit. A man's strengths, gifts, and capabilities are only useful to God to the degree they have been crucified of all self-reliance at Calvary. More often than not, a person's strength serves as God's rival, his ability as Satan's opening.

Paul's own words tell us what the Lord was after: "My strength is made perfect in weakness." God wanted to reveal His strength in Paul's life, but this meant he would have to go through more of the "death-to-self" process. The process of crucifixion is what the Lord uses to weaken the self-life so that He might live through the believer. The life of victory is directly proportional to the degree that a believer's flesh has been put to death. There is not a believer alive today who does not continually need to experience more of this important process.

Our Great Need

For each of these men, their victory was sealed when they saw their own need. No matter what level of spirituality a person may attain in this life, our Redeemer will never be satisfied to leave him there. God always desires better for us. He alone understands the spiritual riches available to the person making the effort to truly seek Him.

Rex Andrews was one of the leaders of the Zion Faith Homes —the ministry I described in Chapter One that made such a deep impression upon my soul. He is one of the few people I know of in this century who certainly broke through to the third plateau described earlier in this chapter. He is a modern-day example of someone the Lord truly conquered.

Rex Andrews was already in God's presence by the time I arrived at the Faith Homes, but I asked one of my friends trained by him what it was like to be around him. "He was in the fire of the Holy Ghost and yet was not self-righteous," he replied. "Mr. Andrews interceded for others for six to seven hours every night for 30 years. Sometimes when I would get out of line as an intern there, he would give me a withering rebuke that would immediately stop me from going astray. Yet, no matter how strong he might be with me, I could never get away from the godly love in those eyes. I could take his reproof because I knew he was pouring out his heart in intercession for me every single night."

The following story properly expresses the point of this chapter. One day, as Rex Andrews led a ministerial training class, he had his interns practicing how to give an altar call. Standing at the podium was a young girl pouring out her heart to an imaginary group of sinners, pleading with them to repent. Right in the middle of her altar call, much to her shock, she looked up to see Mr. Andrews, now in his eighties, rolling his wheelchair toward the altar with tears streaming down his cheeks. "I'm coming, Jesus," he cried. "I'm coming!"

This man lived with such an overwhelming sense of his need for Jesus, that he completely lost track of his surroundings and broke before the Lord. Mr. Andrews, like Job, David, and Paul, learned how to live where all victory begins and ends: at his Master's feet. He found that place because of his unceasing desire to draw close to Him.

Part Two
The God Who Meets Our Needs

Meditation For Today

"We acknowledge that our greatest need is to have a far greater revelation of what You are really like. We ask You to meet that need."[1]

Joy Dawson

"For what higher, more exalted, and more compelling goal can there be than to know God?"[2]

J.I. Packer

"What can we know, without experience, about the character or Spirit of God?"[3]

Charles Finney

"There are two things that never cease to amaze me: How good God is and how evil sin is. The more I come to know God, the more I realize the depths of His goodness are inexhaustible. Likewise, the more I read the papers, the more I realize that there is no end to the potential evil of mankind."

Douglas Detert

"So that you may walk in a manner worthy of the Lord, to please Him in all respects, bearing fruit in every good work and increasing in the knowledge of God."[4]

The Apostle Paul

Chapter Five

Seeking, Knowing and Loving God

Nicholas Herman was raised in France by godly parents who taught him to live for the Lord. As a young man, he joined the army and went off to war. At one point, the Germans captured him, mistaking him for a spy. While interrogating him, they were impressed with his sincere devotion to Christ and released him. He later suffered a severe leg wound that left him disabled for life.

Not until Nick was in his fifties did he decide to give his life completely to the work of the Lord. One day, he presented himself to one of the most prestigious ministries in France, willing to serve in any way he could. Initially, the ministers were impressed with his attitude. Before long they discovered that he was just an ordinary fellow who was not endowed with any special gifts. Consequently, he landed a permanent position washing pots and pans!

Nevertheless, Nick's lack of ability served to make him more aware of his need for his Heavenly Father's daily care. In fact, it was this need that roused within him an unabated passion to know God. "During the hours designated for prayer," he once said, "I meditated on the truth and character of God that we must accept by the light of faith, rather than spending time in laborious meditations and readings. By meditation on Jesus Himself, I advanced in my knowledge of this lovable Person with Whom I resolved to dwell always. Completely immersed in my understanding of God's majesty, I used to shut myself up in the kitchen. There alone, after having done everything that was necessary for my work, I would devote myself to prayer in all the time that was left."[5]

Nick was not a great man, but he sincerely sought a great God. His best friend said, "The love of God reigned so completely in (his) heart that he turned all his affections toward this divine Beloved."[6] Such a fascination for God so gripped his heart that he developed the habit of staying in constant communion with Him throughout the day. "Everything was the same to him—every place, every job. The good brother found God everywhere, as much while he was repairing shoes as while he was praying with the community. He was in no hurry to go on retreats, because he found the same God to love and adore in his ordinary work as in the depth of the desert."[7]

"In this intimate union with the Lord, our brother's passions grew so calm that he scarcely felt them any more. He developed a gentle disposition, complete honesty, and the most charitable heart in the world. His kind face, his gracious and affable air, his simple and modest manner immediately won him the esteem and the good will of everyone who saw him. The more familiar with him they became, the more they became aware of how profoundly upright and reverent he was."[8]

Eventually, as word circulated about Nick, national ministers began calling on him. This humble, yet distinguished, dishwasher was not concerned with impressing them, nor did he desire to make a name for himself. He simply shared his great love for God, as he did with anyone else who showed an interest. One of these ministers, a Catholic bishop, recorded some of these conversations. Shortly after Nick died, the bishop compiled them into a small book treasured by many believers today, *The Practice of the Presence of God*. Nick was entrusted with the menial tasks of washing dishes and repairing shoes. Nevertheless, for more than 300 years Brother Lawrence's (the name he adopted in the monastery) love for God has inspired thousands of seeking hearts. His insights have lasted for over three centuries because he tapped into the most powerful spiritual truth in the kingdom of heaven: the abiding presence of God. Undoubtedly, Brother Lawrence reached level three in his Christian journey (see Graph 4-1, page 49)—deep intimacy with God. His life is a testimony to the fact that despite their lot in life, sincere seekers can experience intimate, unbroken fellowship with the Lord.

While spiritual life is complex, Christianity is clearly defined, from beginning to end, by an individual's relationship to God. An intimate relationship with the Lord comes about through seeking Him; it is developed as our knowledge of God increases, and is brought to full maturity in our love for Him. It is for this very purpose that God created man, and it is the fulfillment of man's greatest need.

When Knowledge Becomes Union

The Bible uses several relational paradigms to illustrate the different aspects of our relationship with God: Father-son, king-subject, master-servant, shepherd-sheep, and husband-wife. These examples teach us how the Father cares for His children, the King rules His subjects, the Shepherd guides His sheep, and the Master treats His bondservants. However, to describe the intimacy He desires to have with man, God uses the husband-wife union as His example. In the other relationships, the authority figures must maintain distance between themselves and their subordinates. When a man becomes intimate with his wife, he establishes a deep spiritual bond unmatched by the fellowship other relationships enjoy. Only a husband and wife were created to be one flesh together.

In Genesis 4:1, we see that "Adam knew Eve." He had sexual intercourse with her. This spiritual union was the first of its kind outside of the presence of God. The sexual experience continues to be the highest form of intimacy between a man and a woman. A husband cannot fully know his wife until he has this experience with her. The knowledge that results from these moments of deep intimacy continually unfolds and grows throughout their marriage, keeping the two people in sync spiritually and emotionally. This act of marital love solidifies their bond and propels the marriage relationship to a pinnacle of expression in which all other human relationships pale in comparison.

By the same token, God greatly desires to know—have intercourse with—His people. Jesus said, "I and the Father are one" (John 10:30). Later, as He prayed for the disciples, He said, "And the

glory which Thou hast given Me I have given to them; that they may
be one, just as We are one; I in them, and Thou in Me, that they may
be perfected in unity, that the world may know that Thou didst send
Me, and didst love them, even as Thou didst love Me" (John 17:22-23).
Paul later made reference to this as well. "Or do you not know that
the one who joins himself to a harlot is one body with her? For He
says, 'The two will become one flesh.' But the one who joins
himself to the Lord is one spirit with Him" (I Corinthians 6:16-17).
Throughout Scripture, our Heavenly Father makes it abundantly
clear that He is a jealous God and that His great passion is to be one
with His people. He is not confused about this, nor has He changed
His mind. He yearns for this now, in a very real and practical way.

Undeniably, love brings greater vulnerability and a more
pronounced pain upon rejection. Sometimes we overemphasize
God's judicial role in our lives to the point that we forget He is a
person. What happens when His children uncaringly spurn His love?

God's Rejected Love

Throughout the Old Testament, God bares His soul and
expresses His deep grief over the unfaithfulness of His backslidden
people. After the people murmured against the Lord, Moses told
them they had "rejected the Lord" (Numbers 11:20). The Psalmist later
reinforced this when he said, "How often they rebelled against Him
in the wilderness, and grieved Him in the desert! And again and
again they tempted God, and pained the Holy One of Israel" (Psalm
78:40-41). The prophets vividly compare God's unfaithful people to,
"well fed, lusty stallions," "a swift she-camel running here and
there," "a donkey in heat," "sniffing the wind in her craving," and
finally, to a prostitute giving herself away to anyone who will have
her. Philip Yancey explains the Lord's response to all of this:

> The powerful image of a jilted lover explains
> why, in his speeches to the prophets, God seems to
> "change his mind" every few seconds. He is preparing
> to obliterate Israel—wait, now he is weeping, holding
> out open arm—no, he is sternly pronouncing judgment
> again. Those shifting moods seem hopelessly irrational,
> except to anyone who has been jilted by a lover.[9]

God the Son suffered the rejection of His people in Old Testament times. Paul tells us He was "the spiritual rock which followed them..." (I Corinthians 10:4). The rejection He suffered became even more personal when He appeared in "the likeness of men" (Philippians 2:7). Jesus said, "The Son of Man must suffer many things, and be rejected by the elders and chief priests and scribes, and be killed, and be raised up on the third day" (Luke 9:22), and later called Himself "the stone which the builders rejected" (Matthew 21:42). Near the end of His woeful life on earth, His pent-up emotions came gushing out as He looked upon His beloved city: "O Jerusalem, Jerusalem, who kills the prophets and stones those who are sent to her! How often I wanted to gather your children together, the way a hen gathers her chicks under her wings, and you were unwilling" (Matthew 23:37). Alexander MacLaren describes our lamenting Savior:

> The parting wail of rejected love. His full heart overflows in that sad cry of lamentation over the long-continued foiling of the efforts of a love that would fain have fondled and defended. What intensity of feeling is in the redoubled naming of the city! How yearningly and wistfully He calls, as if He might still win the faithless one, and how lingeringly unwilling He is to give up hope!...
>
> So the lament passes into the solemn final leave-taking, with which our Lord closes His ministry among the Jews, and departs from the temple... It had been the house of God; now He casts it off and leaves it to them to do as they will with it. The saddest punishment of long-continued rejection of His pleading love is that it ceases at last to plead.[10]

Just prior to this experience, Jesus told a parable in an attempt to prick the hearts of His people. Again, the same picture is painted: the gracious offer, the hard-hearted response.

> The kingdom of heaven may be compared to a king, who gave a wedding feast for his son. And he sent out his slaves to call those who had been invited

to the wedding feast, and they were unwilling to come. Again he sent out other slaves saying, "Tell those who have been invited, 'Behold, I have prepared my dinner; my oxen and my fattened livestock are all butchered and everything is ready; come to the wedding feast.'" But they paid no attention and went their way, one to his own farm, another to his business, and the rest seized his slaves and mistreated them and killed them.

But the king was enraged and sent his armies, and destroyed those murderers, and set their city on fire. Then he said to his slaves, "The wedding is ready, but those who were invited were not worthy. Go therefore to the main highways, and as many as you find there, invite to the wedding feast." And those slaves went out into the streets, and gathered together all they found, both evil and good; and the wedding hall was filled with dinner guests (Matthew 22:2-10).

We sense the mounting passion rising within Jesus before He pronounced judgment on the house of Israel. "Behold, your house is being left to you desolate!" (Matthew 23:38). Nothing incites anger like unrequited love; the deeper the love extended, the greater the fury when rejected. The saga of man's apathetic response to God's love is a 6,000 year-old narrative of immense sadness. Despite God 's continued attempts to extend mercy and be a husband to His people, very few respond to His love.

The Great Commandment

Jesus said, "You shall love the Lord your God with all your heart, and with all your soul, and with all your mind" (Matthew 22:37). The increasing passivity and lukewarmness in today's Church allows little emphasis on this all-important commandment, if any at all. Many pastors prefer to pacify and appease their congregations rather than fearlessly insist that the people thoroughly examine their hearts to determine if they walk obediently to the Word.

People are flippant with this commandment because they do not really understand the word love. Accustomed to using love to describe their affectionate feelings for sports teams, jobs, and family pets, many people honestly believe they also love the Lord. Excessive use of the word has gutted it of its real meaning. The Greek word *agape* connotes a much stronger devotion than our English translation. Agape demands daily companionship, friendship, and communication—precisely what many lack in their devotion to God. The depth and passion of true agape love is expressed in Jesus' words, "You shall love the Lord your God with all your heart, and with all your soul, and with all your mind."

Many believers' love for God reminds me of the story of a young man who greatly loved a certain girl. After dating several months, they were married. On their wedding night, longing to fully express his love to his new bride through physical intimacy, he was sorely disappointed when she rebuffed his efforts saying she was not in the mood. "She must be nervous," he thought to himself in patient understanding. However, after several years of constant rejection, he finally lashed out her. "This marriage is a sham! You don't love me! In fact, you're not even interested in me! Why did you marry me?" Would you say that he is just over-reacting or being selfish? Absolutely not!

I wonder if the Lord feels this way about people who claim to love Him but have hearts far from Him. Has their marriage ever been consummated? Do they keep their Bridegroom at bay, or respond to His love with indifference? I believe God never intended such a thing to happen. The Lord desires the kind of relationship in which two people become one, sharing their deepest secrets with each other—a union cemented together through a deep devotion to each other.

Is it cruel or unusual for God to expect a reciprocal response to His love? I can best answer that question by describing the relationship I have with my wife Kathy. She came from a close, loving family where each child knew that their mother and father loved each other and each of them. My family, on the other hand, was the opposite. I was raised in a home where affection was never expressed. When Kathy and I married, I assumed we would live together and at the same time maintain our own separate lives. Was I ever mistaken! She would not stand for a distant relationship! From the beginning, she was completely committed to me and expected the same devotion in return. God demands that believers love Him with all their heart, soul, and mind. He has the right to demand that kind of love from us because He loves us in that way.

Loving God Equates With Seeking Him

We must express our love for God, who is a spirit being, in a different sort of way than we do with people. I love my wife through an occasional touch on the shoulder, an affirming smile, or by being nice to her. We cannot do this in the same way with the Lord, however. He does expect us to pay attention to Him and to include Him in our lives throughout each day. He expects us to express our love to Him on a regular basis. Even though we cannot show physical love to the Lord, we can still demonstrate our love for Him as we worship Him in spirit and truth.

This is the tremendous spiritual truth which Brother Lawrence tapped into. *The Practice of the Presence of God* was not written as a "how-to" book. It was just a simple Christian brother sharing about his daily intercourse with God. Regardless of the task at hand, he made the Lord a part of his minute-by-minute existence. His life is an example of what it means to love the Lord.

This kind of devotion to God requires that we seek the Lord. This divine mandate spans the entire length and breadth of Scripture. Moses said, "But from there you will seek the LORD your God, and you will find Him if you search for Him with all your heart and all your soul" (Deuteronomy 4:29). David said, "Glory in His holy name; let the heart of those who seek the LORD be glad. Seek the LORD and His strength; seek His face continually" (I Chronicles 16:10-11). Isaiah said, "Seek the LORD while He may be found; call upon Him while He is near" (Isaiah 55:6). Hosea said, "Break up your fallow ground, for it is time to seek the LORD until He comes to rain righteousness on you" (Hosea 10:12). And Zephaniah added, "Seek the LORD, all you humble of the earth who have carried out His ordinances; seek righteousness, seek humility. Perhaps you will be hidden in the day of the LORD'S anger" (Zephaniah 2:3).

A.W. Tozer, bemoaning the apathy of our age, wrote the following:

In the midst of this great chill there are some,
I rejoice to acknowledge, who will not be content with

shallow logic. They will admit the force of the argument (that seeking God is only for spiritual teachers), and then turn away with tears to hunt some lonely place and pray, "O God, show me thy glory." They want to taste, to touch with their hearts, to see with their inner eyes the wonder that is God.

I want deliberately to encourage this mighty longing after God. The lack of it has brought us to our present low estate. The stiff and wooden quality about our religious lives is a result of our lack of holy desire. Complacency is a deadly foe of all spiritual growth. Acute desire must be present or there will be no manifestation of Christ to His people. He waits to be wanted. Too bad that with many of us He waits so long, so very long, in vain.

Every age has its own characteristics. Right now we are in an age of religious complexity. The simplicity which is in Christ is rarely found among us. In its stead are programs, methods, organizations and a world of nervous activities which occupy time and attention but can never satisfy the longing of the heart. The shallowness of our inner experience, the hollowness of our worship, and that servile imitation of the world which marks our promotional methods all testify that we, in this day, know God only imperfectly, and the peace of God scarcely at all.[11]

Only a genuine love for God drives a person to seek after Him with all his heart. A great reward awaits the treasure hunter of a Being who desires to be sought after: the knowledge of God Himself. This is the life of victory that takes the believer out of the slums of mediocrity!

Meditation For Today

"God loves us; not because we are lovable but because He is love, not because he needs to receive but because He delights to give...

"Though our feelings come and go, His love for us does not. It is not wearied by our sins, or our indifference; and, therefore, it is quite relentless in its determination that we shall be cured of those sins, at whatever cost to us, at whatever cost to Him...

"In awful and surprising truth, we are the objects of His love. You asked for a loving God: you have one... (God's love is) not a senile benevolence that drowsily wishes you to be happy in your own way, not the cold philanthropy of a conscientious magistrate, not the care of a host who feels responsible for the comfort of his guests, but the consuming fire Himself, the Love that made the worlds...

"...He is not proud, He stoops to conquer, He will have us even though we have shown that we prefer everything else to Him, and come to Him because there is 'nothing better' now to be had."[1]

C.S. Lewis

"Believer, look back through all thine experience, and think of the way whereby the Lord thy God has led thee in the wilderness, and how He hath fed and clothed thee every day — how He hath borne with thine ill manners — how He hath put up with all thy murmurings, and all thy longings for the flesh-pots of Egypt — how He has opened the rock to supply thee, and fed thee with manna that came down from heaven. Think of how His grace has been sufficient for thee in all thy troubles — how His blood has been a pardon to thee in all thy sins — how His rod and His staff have comforted thee. When thou hast thus looked back upon the love of the Lord, then let faith survey His love in the future, for remember that Christ's covenant and blood have something more in them than in the past. He who has loved thee and pardoned thee, shall never cease to love and pardon... Surely as we meditate on 'the love of the Lord,' our hearts burn within us, and we long to love Him more."[2]

C.H. Spurgeon

Chapter Six

The Essence of the Holy Spirit

Mankind is born into a chaotic, fallen world and is programmed for lawlessness. This propensity to sin puts every soul at a disadvantage—each of us are spiritually bankrupt from day one. Humanity's awful condition is not based upon socioeconomic status. The nature of sin causes the hearts of the rich and poor alike to become progressively worse over time. Divine intervention is the only remedy.

After imparting life to one who has been spiritually dead in trespasses and sins (Ephesians 2:1), the Holy Spirit remains intimately and intricately involved in the believer's life, convicting him of "sin and righteousness and judgment." (John 16:8) One of the first steps toward living in victory requires a willingness to submit to and be led by the Spirit of God. This requires trust. Just as a patient must willingly lay down on the operating table at the mercy of the scalpel-wielding surgeon, so must a believer yield himself and entrust his life into the skillful hands of the Chief Surgeon of souls so that a deep inward work may be accomplished.

In the Old Testament, the Spirit is revealed to us through the word *ruach*, which "refers to the atmosphere, especially the wind, which is an invisible, irresistible power, sometimes benign and beneficial, sometimes raging and destructive."[3] The New Testament word *pneuma* is typically used in the Greek to describe wind or breath.

The Holy Spirit is a Person—a Force and an Influence existing in a realm separate from but concurrent with our own. He exists in the eternal but operates in the temporal. While He is one of the three Persons of the Godhead, He cannot be limited to our finite concept of what that means. He is a Person who proceeds from the Father and yet, at the same time, He is also the essential being of what God is (in some way we cannot here and now comprehend).

The Bible describes God's make-up in three ways. First, Jesus said, "God is Spirit" (John 4:24). Secondly, we are told, "God is a consuming fire" (Hebrews 12:29). And lastly, the apostle John said, "God is love," or more accurately, "God is *agape*" (I John 4:8, 16). Transposed into an algebraical equation, it would look something like this:

God=Spirit
God=A Consuming Fire
God=Agape

Any math student knows that if a=b and a=c and a=d, then b=c and b=d. Using the substitution principle, the following equality exists:

God=Spirit
Spirit=A Consuming Fire
Spirit=Agape

What is revealed here about the Holy Spirit? He is a consuming fire and He is agape. These three characterizations of God are simply different perspectives of the same thing. He appeared to one as a Spirit, appeared to another as a consuming fire, and appeared to another as agape. I propose to you that the Holy Spirit is a consuming fire of love.

We hear people say things like, "That man has a bitter spirit," or "That woman has a critical spirit," or "That guy has a spirit of lust." It seems that different spirits manifest themselves through different ungodly passions. The Holy Spirit is the personification of this passion which is called agape in the Greek. Just as a demon can be so filled with a passion for sex that he actually becomes a spirit of lust, God is so closely identified with agape that He is agape. John did not tell us that God has it or created it, but that God is agape.

Agape is the Spirit that God is in and this Spirit is a consuming fire. The word love is not a clear representation for the word agape. There are three other Greek terms that are also translated as love in the English language. *Eros* is sexual love, *phileo* is brotherly love, and *storge* describes the sense of deep commitment two people feel toward each other. These all, for the most part, represent human emotions. Not only does the English word encompass all of these Greek terms but many more. The fact of the matter is that we use the word love very loosely.

Our misuse of the word love has distorted the true meaning of the Greek word agape. Agape represents a very strong and powerful passion. This is in stark contrast to our comparatively anemic use of the word love.

Allow me to illustrate. Peter walks by Carl's house and flicks a cigarette butt into his yard. We would say Carl is irritated by Peter's actions. What if Peter deliberately brought a full garbage can into Carl's yard and dumped it from one end of the yard to the other? We would safely characterize his emotion as extreme anger, or even rage.

Let's look at another illustration. Shirley is nervous when she sees a strange looking man walk by her house. What would describe her emotions if he ran toward her with a knife in his hand? Horror and terror might be accurate descriptions.

When making a distinction between our idea of love and the actual meaning of the word agape, we are talking about one word that can mean nothing more than a mild affection and the other word which describes a driving passion. It is this fervor that one could express as a consuming fire.

Agape describes the essence of the Holy Spirit. For the purposes of this book, we will examine further the Bible's own definition of agape found in I Corinthians 13. But first, let's go back to our equation. If the Bible says that God is Spirit and God is agape, then we would not be too far off the mark if we substituted the word agape with the word God—or even with the term Holy Spirit, would we? With that in mind, let's take a few verses in what has become known as "the love chapter" and use them as descriptions of what the Holy Spirit is like.

> The Holy Spirit is longsuffering,
> He is kind,
> He is not jealous;
> The Holy Spirit does not brag and is not arrogant,
> nor does He act unbecomingly;
> The Holy Spirit does not seek His own,
> He is not provoked,
> and does not take into account a wrong suffered,
> The Holy Spirit does not rejoice in unrighteousness,
>   but rejoices with the truth;
> He bears all things, believes all things, hopes all
>   things, endures all things.
> The Holy Spirit never fails.

With this as our blueprint, perhaps we can gain a fresh understanding about this Spirit who desires to work in our lives.

Longsuffering

Listed as one of the qualities of a person filled with the Holy Spirit (Galatians 5:22), patience is one of those virtues that does not receive the esteem it deserves. We joke about God teaching us patience, but few really seem to appreciate how vital it is for the life of the believer.

Strong's Dictionary defines *makrothumeo* as "to be long-spirited, i.e. (obj.) forbearing or (subj.) patient—bear (suffer) long, be longsuffering, have (long) patience, be patient, patiently endure."[4] It is not simply that the Lord is willing to suffer—and suffer He does—but that He has the ability and willingness to suffer long.

Another dictionary says, "Longsuffering is that quality of self-restraint in the face of provocation which does not hastily retaliate or promptly punish; it is the opposite of anger and is associated with mercy, and is used of God..."[5] This is why the Lord calls Himself "slow to anger" (Exodus 34:6). When provoked, the Lord does not respond out of the highly charged emotions of the moment, like we humans tend to do. His response is slow, measured, and calculated, and it always goes through the Holy Spirit's filter of love. God is not like the person who says, "I don't get mad, I just get even." He does not get mad or even, at least not in the petulant way humans do.

Matthew Henry grasped the very motive behind the longsuffering character of God when he said: "It can endure evil and provocation, without being filled with resentment or revenge. It will put up with many slights from the person it loves, and wait long to see the kindly effects of such patience on him."[6]

For this Being of Love, patiently enduring the abuse of those whom His affections are set upon is simply an unavoidable part of trying to convey that love. In fact, it is not simply something He wishes He could avoid, but is willing to endure; it is something He does joyfully. It is His loving and patient response to our rebellion that makes us love Him all the more. In a sense, He is happy to put up with our slights, knowing one day we will recognize how we have treated Him and it will only serve to increase our love for Him. "But God demonstrates His own love toward us, in that while we were yet sinners, Christ died for us" (Romans 5:8).

Had He created religion with the cut-and-dried mandate that either we serve Him or go to hell, people would serve Him through false motives. He would be like a dictator surrounded by "yes men" living in terror of displeasing their president, serving him with an outward loyalty.

In this scenario, our Dictator came and laid down His life for us, taking our abuse then and ever since, continually asking us to join Him in a love relationship. His willingness to endure whatever we may shell out and to wait as long as it takes is proof of His preeminent devotion to us. As one said, "If Jesus doesn't love us, what meaneth these nail prints in His hands?"

Kind

When I think of kindness, a former co-worker named Wilda comes to mind. She was one of the nicest people I have ever known.

Since she was also a Jehovah's Witness, I think it safe to assume that her kindness was not of the Lord. She simply had a pleasant and kind disposition.

When we think of biblical terms such as love, patience, and kindness, we tend to fit those terms into definitions that coincide with our own experiences. When we try to define characteristics of Almighty God in terms we can only relate to with imperfect humans, our definitions tend to be shallow and empty.

Is God kind like Wilda was kind? Certainly, just like He is powerful like Mike Tyson is powerful. Our kindness is shallow compared to God's burning love for people.

We all have stories of little kindnesses God has done for us. I have a statement I often say to others: "No kind thing the Lord does for people surprises me." It's true! I have become familiar with Him to the point of being accustomed to seeing His little kindnesses to those around me. I have come to expect His kindnesses in my life and in the lives of others.

Someone said, "The Lord has never had a bad thought toward you." I know this to be the case. He is simply not the angry judge I pictured Him to be. The Lord is kind. He is looking to help and to save. This is the Spirit He lives in.

Is Not Jealous Or Arrogant And Does Not Brag

If it was not so sad, it would probably be comical to us to see how we must look to God. Inflated and swollen with our own sense of importance, we humans must be a pathetic sight indeed! We are unlike the Lord in so many ways.

God has a lowly disposition and is not easily seen by prideful and petty-minded humans. One clear contrast between the Lord and humans occurred the night before Jesus was crucified when His disciples argued about which of them was the greatest. Jesus responded to them by saying, "whoever wishes to become great among you shall be your servant, and whoever wishes to be first among you shall be your slave; just as the Son of Man did not come to be served, but to serve..." (Matthew 20:26-28).

One of the problems we have connecting with the Lord in a real way is that we have a hard time finding Him! The Lord is God Almighty, the Alpha and Omega, the Ancient of Days, Jehovah

Jireh, and the Mighty One of Israel. These names describe His majesty and His power, but He takes the form of a servant nevertheless.

In a certain way, He reminds me of the janitor who won the lotto and bought a mega-corporation. From the beginning he just could not seem to fit into the boardroom scene. Every time the vice-presidents went to get a signature or his approval on some acquisition, they inevitably found him in the basement mopping floors and scrubbing toilets!

The reason He is not jealous or arrogant and does not brag is simply because He is extremely humble.

Does Not Act Unbecomingly

There was a gentle, unselfish quality about Jesus that attracted people. He had a sweet Spirit.

How unlike Jesus is a man I know pictured on the cover of a national magazine screaming at abortion rights advocates. The news photographer was happy to show such a mean-spirited representative of Christianity. The truth is that this man cared very little about those unborn babies. He was concerned about being right and making others see things the way he saw them. Abortion is very wrong, but the way to win the battle against this evil in our country is not to act like the devil.

Christians often fail to properly represent the Lord. Unlike the way we sometimes act, the Lord never acts in an unseemly manner. He is gentle and kind by nature.

Does Not Seek His Own

All sin begins with wanting something for self. A man wants the thrill of illicit sex and gets involved in an affair. Another loses his temper and screams at a driver who cuts him off in traffic. A cashier slips a few dollars into her purse every night as she closes the store. A teenager seethes with bitterness as she loses the last cheerleading spot to another girl. It is all sin, motivated by wanting something for self. This is the nature of man.

The nature of God is much different. He is not in a spirit of "getting" for self but in a spirit of giving. "For God so loved the world He gave..." (John 3:16). In a sense, it is the only thing the Lord knows how to do. Giving is part of His nature. What else does someone who is utterly selfless do?

One of the best human illustrations of what goes on inside the heart of God is the final image of Scrooge. After three frightening encounters with "ghosts" from the past, present and future, he is a transformed man. The movie ends with a beaming Scrooge giving out gifts to everybody he meets. This is a small (earthly) picture of the selfless heart of God.

Is Not Provoked And Does Not Take Into Account A Wrong Suffered

The Lord does not get provoked to anger because He does not get offended. Jesus is the best example of this. He was arrested, beaten, mocked, flogged, and finally, nailed to the cross. Satan did everything within his power to get Jesus to rise up in a retaliatory spirit. But Jesus never did. He went to the cross praying for those who were killing Him.

When I was in Bible school, a group of students gathered to watch a movie about the life of Christ. During the part of the movie where Jesus was being beaten and mocked, one of the students blurted out, "How humiliating that must have been!" I responded, "It wasn't humiliating to Jesus because He had no pride."

Being humiliated by someone only hurts when a person's pride is wounded. If there is no pride, there is nothing there to be crushed. Jesus was not provoked to retaliation because He has no pride.

Does Not Rejoice In Unrighteousness But With The Truth

Rejoicing with unrighteousness refers to gloating over the downfall of an enemy. "Do I have any pleasure in the death of the wicked," declares the Lord GOD, "rather than that he should turn from his ways and live?" (Ezekiel 18:23). The Lord does not rejoice in seeing man suffer the consequences for his sin, no matter how much he deserves it. He does not rejoice in seeing anyone perish, no matter how evil they have been. He does not rejoice in seeing people go to Hell, no matter how much they rebelled. The Lord wants to give life and does to all who are interested.

One aspect of judgment can be illustrated from our own court system. For a period of time, I served as a bailiff in the Criminal Courts Building in Los Angeles. Sometimes we saw a defendant to whom, for whatever reason, the judge clearly wanted to extend mercy. Under pressure from the taxpayers, the California legislature had enacted mandatory sentencing guidelines. Even if a judge wanted to release a criminal, the guidelines forced a particular sentence.

In the same manner, God's justice system requires that unrepentant sinners be sentenced to hell, no matter how much pity He feels for them. Even though love longs to show kindness, perfect holiness demands justice. Hell is a place for those who have shown they do not want to live in the kingdom of God. As C.S. Lewis said, "I willingly believe that the damned are, in one sense, successful rebels to the end; that the doors of hell are locked on the inside."[7]

Bears All Things

The truth of this profound statement can hardly be comprehended. Do you know that the Lord bears you? That means that He is under you, in a sense, holding you up, helping you make it through. The poem "Footprints" is an accurate portrayal of this.

Physically, God bears the entire world. The Bible says, "...in Him all things hold together" (Colossians 1:17) and that He "...upholds all things by the word of His power" (Hebrews 1:3).

Even more than that, He spiritually bears His children. David said, "Blessed be the Lord, who daily bears our burden, the God who is our salvation" (Psalms 68:19). He also said, "The Lord is the sustainer of my soul" (Psalms 54:4) and that it is He "who keeps us in life" (Psalms 66:8).

The Lord bears our burdens in a way that we do not understand. He is under us, lifting us up, and keeping us from falling.

Believes All Things, Hopes All Things, Endures All Things

The Lord's thinking is opposite of the thinking of the cynic, who only sees failure or the criticizer who only sees fault. The Lord believes the best about His children. Put another way, He believes in us.

The Lord does not write people off because they fail or disobey. He simply keeps trying to help them and encourage them.

The reason He can think that way is He does not have a knowledge of good and evil in the same way we do. To put it simply, the Holy Spirit is innocent. He is omniscient, but He doesn't have the intimate knowledge of evil that comes from experience. An illustration of this is a child who looks into a bar and sees fighting, arguing, laughing, and all the other behavior that goes along with drinking. He sees what is going on, but because he has never been in the spirit of it, he does not really understand it. It's perplexing to him. He understands the drinking in a certain way, but he lacks intimate knowledge of it. In many ways the Lord is like a child. He has an innocence about Him that you see in the face of a small child.

Perhaps because He only knows the good in this way, He is able to believe and hope the best for people. He has a sunny and cheerful view of life and man. How else could He handle all the death and destruction He must witness everyday? He sees a brighter future when the days of man finally (and mercifully) come to an end and the day of the Lord begins. The Holy Spirit sees the beginning from the end and knows that there is a wonderful future laid up for His loved ones. His hope is based in His knowledge of the eternal. This helps explain why He is able to endure seeing so much evil.

Never Fails

It is a wonderful thing to know that God is there. Many men know this in their minds but not yet in their hearts. That kind of assurance grows as we experience God's presence in times of distress.

One memory of God's faithfulness is the time I appeared on The Oprah Winfrey Show. The producers wanted a guest who had been involved in sexual addiction for a show they were about to air. They flew me out to Chicago, had me picked up at the airport by a limousine, and put me up in a suite at the Hilton. The show was to be taped the next morning.

Appearing on television was new and overwhelming. That entire night I fretted and worried. I could not sleep, so I paced back and forth in my room, pleading with God to help me. The next morning, I was taken to the studio. I felt absolutely worn out and exhausted right up until I walked onto the set, when suddenly, I felt invigorated! In one instant, I was transformed from a state of weariness and fear to alert confidence. He has done this sort of thing for me so many times now that I no longer fear; I know He is already awaiting me in the upcoming situation.

    The Lord loves us and will never fail us.

    Receiving a fresh revelation about what the Lord is really like will go a long way in helping us to make a greater surrender to Him. The life of victory cannot be attained without a life of surrender.

    In this chapter we have seen the loving nature of the Lord, but this is only half the picture! God is love, but if He never did anything with that love what use would it be? It is time now to learn about His tender mercies.

Meditation For Today

"How great is Thy goodness, which Thou hast stored up
for those who fear Thee, which Thou hast wrought for those who
take refuge in Thee, before the sons of men!
    "Thy lovingkindness, O LORD, extends to the heavens,
Thy faithfulness reaches to the skies."[1]
                                        David

Great Is Thy Faithfulness
"Great is Thy faithfulness, O God my Father,
There is no shadow of turning with Thee;
Thou changest not, Thy compassions, they fail not;
As Thou hast been Thou forever wilt be.

Summer and winter, and springtime and harvest,
Sun, moon, and stars in their courses above
Join with all nature in manifold witness
To Thy great faithfulness, mercy and love.

Pardon for sin and a peace that endureth,
Thine own dear presence to cheer and to guide;
Strength for today and bright hope for tomorrow,
Blessings all mine, with ten thousand beside!

Chorus
Great Is Thy faithfulness! Great is Thy faithfulness!
Morning by morning new mercies I see;
All I have needed Thy hand hath provided;
Great is Thy faithfulness, Lord unto me!"[2]
                                        Thomas Chisholm

Chapter Seven

The God of Mercy

If the essence of God is love, as we've set forth here, it stands to reason that all of His dealings with mankind issue forth from His love. The following illustration helps us see it more clearly:

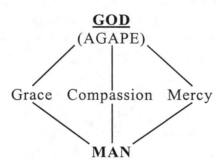

Intrinsically, God is pure love. He bestows His love on every living soul. His amazing grace for our sin comes through this love. Such love moves Him to show compassion for our problems and to extend the mercy required to meet our needs. This chapter will focus on God's mercy. Let's begin by looking at two other expressions of the Lord's love for us.

Grace

God desires intimate, unbroken fellowship with us. However, a wide gulf exists between the two. God is holy, pure, and righteous in all His ways. This places Him in direct opposition to anything that resembles pride or self-centeredness. In His heavenly realm, there are no spots or blemishes—there is no sin because everything conforms perfectly to His will.

In stark contrast, man is unholy, impure, and exceedingly sinful—at odds with the Spirit of God. By nature, man is a transgressor. Sin is attached to almost everything he does. Habitually caught in sinful behavior, he is guilty of pride, selfishness, and rebellion against God. The prophet Jeremiah poignantly described the heart of man as being "deceitful above all things, and desperately wicked..." (Jeremiah 17:9). The prognosis of fallen humanity is the same as for the patient diagnosed with a malignant form of cancer spreading throughout his body: imminent death, unless God intervenes.

It is mind-boggling that God, always in the spirit of agape, longs to unite Himself with man. He passionately pursues sinners because He knows us and remembers that we are but dust (Psalm 103:14). As much as any bridegroom on his wedding night, the Lord wants to be one with His Bride. The perfect picture of this passion, if you can read it without blushing, is found in the Song of Solomon. This poetic narrative portrays God's unbridled love for His Beloved.

To really appreciate God's dilemma, imagine a man who loves a woman with all his heart and is prepared to lay his life down for her—for richer or poorer. Wonder of wonders, she agrees to marry him! But he notices something wrong before she makes it to the altar. As she makes her way up the aisle, she glances seductively at other men in the congregation. How inappropriate. What an embarrassment. Obviously she has a divided heart. She is in quite a predicament: she has agreed to marry the groom, but all those other men have suddenly grabbed her attention. What is she to do?

She decides to go through with it. To his amazement, the marriage goes well at first. She sincerely seems committed to the marriage. After a few months though, she starts staying out late. One night, he discovers his worst fears: she has been sleeping around.

She expresses sorrow and asks for his forgiveness, but she

continues having affairs. Repeatedly he catches her lying about her actions. At times, she really does seem to love him, just not enough to change her behavior. How long should he put up with it? How many times must he look the other way or bury his head in the sand? How many apologies should he accept before he divorces her? Hosea understood extending mercy to an unfaithful spouse.

God cannot help Himself. His love drives Him relentlessly toward the object of His desire. It does not matter how often He is hurt. He loves her. It isn't enough that He is willing to accept her back after her repeated failures. When she comes home, He has a loving, welcoming smile on His face. He is happy to see her back, making an effort to stay in the relationship. This is grace: God's unmerited favor toward sinners who are unfaithful by nature. We serve a gracious God who forgives when we humbly ask for it and extends grace to the repentant one. This is good news for bad people!

Compassion

God's compassion takes it a step further. He not only welcomes the repentant, wayward wife home with a smile, but He also has compassion on her addiction to adultery.* He sees her struggle. She wants to do right. She wants to be in this relationship, and yet she continually caves in to the pressures of temptation. He feels badly about her struggle.

A compassionate person sees the needs of others and is moved within. When he sees someone hurting, he can hardly contain himself, becoming so overwhelmed with emotion. He cries out to God and is unsatisfied until the need is met.

The Lord is full of compassion toward us. His compassions move Him to do good to us and to meet our needs.

Such compassion is expressed in the story Jesus told of the Good Samaritan. The Samaritan was moved with compassion, but the priest and Levite passed by on the other side of the road (Luke 11:31-32). The Lord never ignores us when we are in need. He never crosses the road to avoid our problems. He sees our needs and is

---

* We must be careful not to get the wrong impression that a holy God winks at sin. He feels for our struggle, but He provides a way of escape which He expects us to take.

moved toward them in order to relieve, heal, and restore us.

Mercy

Mercy is living out the love of God. The Old Testament Hebrew word translated mercy in the King James Bible is *hhesed.* It is translated as "lovingkindness" in the NASB and "unfailing love" in the NIV. Hhesed primarily refers to the supply system God established on this earth to meet needs: physical, emotional, and spiritual. As one brother stated:

> Mercy is the radiation of love. Just as there is but one sun in our skies and yet endless rays from our sun, so there are ENDLESS MERCIES from the holy fire of divine love, a love which can never be extinguished...
>
> If we are hungry, mercy is food. If we are thirsty, mercy is water. If we are cold, mercy is warmth and heat and shelter and clothing. If we are discouraged, mercy is encouragement and strength. If we are rebellious, mercy is repentance. If we are guilty (and repent), mercy is pardon. If we are defeated, mercy is victory.[3]

In short, mercy is love in action. Mercy is the natural response of someone who *does* love to another. What is the benefit of unexpressed love? How would our lives be impacted if God only said that He loved us from heaven but never showed it? It wouldn't be a pretty picture. Thank God for His need-filling mercies.

Grace is the welcoming smile of God. Compassion is the natural response of God toward needs. Mercy is the provision for that need. Biblical illustrations may help us to see it more clearly.

On one occasion, Jesus was in a remote area of northern Galilee where He taught the multitudes for several days. This spiritually starved crowd was momentarily seized by His wonderful words of life. Jesus saw their physical needs as well: "I feel compassion for the multitude because they have remained with Me now three days and have nothing to eat" (Matthew 15:32). Even though they didn't deserve His kindness, He looked upon them with compassion and did something. He fed them.

Another time, Jesus was walking along when a leper came to Him pleading for mercy. "And moved with compassion, He stretched out His hand, and touched him, and said to him, I am willing; be cleansed.' And immediately the leprosy left him and he was cleansed" (Luke 5:13). Again, Jesus *saw* the need, *had compassion* on the man, and did the deed of mercy.

On another occasion, Jesus noticed a funeral procession with a mother grieving over her deceased son. "And when the Lord saw her, He felt compassion for her, and said to her, 'Do not weep.' And He came up and touched the coffin, and the bearers came to a halt. And He said, 'Young man, I say to you, arise!' And the dead man sat up, and began to speak. And Jesus gave him back to his mother" (Luke 7:13-15). In each story we find the same ingredients: grace, compassion, and mercy.

God looked down on sinful man with compassion. He loved us. He knew that a perfect sacrifice would be required for our atonement. Despite the pain it caused Him, He did the only thing He could do to meet the need. He sent His precious Son to take our sin on Himself and to die in our place—the greatest mercy ever done. It was all grace for Him to do this for sinful mankind. His compassion gave Him no alternative.

Lloyd John Oglivie clearly has a sight of this:

> Kindness (hhesed) is the steadfast love of the Lord in action toward those who fail. Throughout the Old Testament the words for 'steadfast love,' 'mercy,' and 'kindness' are used interchangeably. Kindness is the persistent effort of the Lord to reach His people and enable them to return to Him.
>
> Jesus Christ was kindness incarnate. He came to express it; lived to model it; died to offer it; and returns to impart it to us in the Holy Spirit.[4]

Indeed, Jesus' ministry involved meeting whatever needs He encountered, constantly giving, sacrificing, and serving others for their good. He never promoted Himself. He simply lived in a passion to do good wherever He had opportunity.

Hebrews 13 says that Jesus was the exact expression or representation of God's nature. Jesus was God in human form doing exactly what God willed to do on earth as in heaven. If you want to know what God is like, simply study the life of Jesus. He was God's revelation of Himself to mankind. God is the changeless one—the same yesterday, today and forever. There is no difference between the God we read about in the Old Testament and the God of the New Testament. Jesus said, "Truly, truly, I say to you, the Son can do nothing of Himself, unless it is something He sees the Father doing; for whatever the Father does, these things the Son also does in like manner. For the Father loves the Son, and shows Him all things that He Himself is doing; and greater works than these will He show Him, that you may marvel" (John 5:19-20).

Throughout the ages man has wondered what God is like. All through His Word the Lord reveals His nature as being good and merciful. God, through Jesus, demonstrated His immense love for all of us on the Cross by taking ownership of our crimes and paying the penalty so that we could go free. Again, if you want to know what activity is ever going on in heaven, look to the life of Jesus. Mercy is the force of life in the kingdom of God.

Doubting God

Unfortunately, after all He did to show His lovingkindness to us, we find it difficult to believe that this is the way God really is. The struggle to believe the best about God goes all the way back to the beginning.

For a time Adam and Eve enjoyed life in their earthly paradise. They were in perfect fellowship and communion with a loving God. Using forbidden fruit, a damnable intruder crept in and poisoned Eve's mind with lies about her Creator. She had avoided this fruit because it was off-limits. How did the devil get her to do it? He made the subtle suggestion that he still uses today: "God isn't really good. He's holding out on you! He's going to make you do something you don't want to do. You can't trust Him. He will hurt you, take things from you, and force you to submit to His will. It is much safer not to put all your trust in Him and go your own way in life."

What a scandal and a shame! Our heavenly Father wants to help, bless, do good, meet needs, and most of all have a love relationship with His children. What does He receive in return? Skepticism, doubt, unbelief, false accusations, and outright rebellion! Yet, in infinite patience, He continues to reach out, make Himself vulnerable, to do good, and to simply hand out favors unconditionally to the undeserving.

Why do we refuse to believe the best about God? There are a number of reasons.

First, we imagine that God is a bigger version of us. It's unthinkable that anyone could possibly be full of goodness. We find it difficult to expand our concepts outside of our own experience. We cannot comprehend an eternal Being. We cannot imagine an infinite, all-powerful, and all-knowing God. It is the same with His intrinsic goodness. We just cannot imagine anyone being that good.

Second, we are so blinded by our own goodness that when we hear the Bible speak of God's goodness it doesn't really affect us. The word goodness (like the word love) has been gutted of its real meaning by our own shallow concept of what it is. We gauge goodness based on how we view ourselves.

A third reason that we have such a poor sight of God's character is because of what the Bible says about His wrath and judgments. Chapter Eight explores these truths.

Finally, we simply do not see His mercy in our daily lives. He does so many things that we do not realize He has done. Many other acts of kindness are missed because our eyes of faith have not been sufficiently opened to see His work in our lives.

The nature of God is riddled with goodness! He is infinitely good. A man who has walked closely with Him cannot help but see that reality. Read what some of the saints of the Bible have proclaimed concerning the Lord:

> Moses said, "The LORD is slow to anger and abundant in lovingkindness... He is God, the faithful God, who keeps His covenant and His lovingkindness to a thousandth generation with those who love Him and keep His commandments;" (Numbers 14:18; Deuteronomy 7:9).

> David, who probably had a better sight of God's nature than anyone else, said, "Thy compassion and

Thy lovingkindnesses, for they have been from of old... All the paths of the LORD are lovingkindness and truth to those who keep His covenant and His testimonies... For Thou, Lord, art good, and ready to forgive, and abundant in lovingkindness to all who call upon Thee... The LORD is gracious and merciful; slow to anger and great in lovingkindness... The LORD is good to all, and His mercies are over all His works" (Psalms 25:6, 10; 86:5; 145:8-9).

Solomon said, "O LORD, the God of Israel, there is no God like Thee in heaven above or on earth beneath, who art keeping covenant and showing lovingkindness to Thy servants who walk before Thee with all their heart" (I Kings 8:23).

And finally Paul said, "But God, being rich in mercy, because of His great love with which He loved us, even when we were dead in our transgressions, made us alive together with Christ (by grace you have been saved), and raised us up with Him, and seated us with Him in the heavenly places, in Christ Jesus, in order that in the ages to come He might show the surpassing riches of His grace in kindness toward us in Christ Jesus" (Ephesians 2:4-7).

This is only a small taste of what Scripture says about the Lord. Each one of these people had a sight of God's nature and a revelation of how He treats mankind.

Mercy In Our Daily Life

A friend of mine says that for every mercy we see God do, He does a thousand others we do not see. As I grow closer to Jesus and learn more about His ways, I see this to be true.

Recently, Kathy and I were staying in a travel trailer in a campground on Cape Cod. We were in the New England area for several months of meetings. We kept the same routine every week: we stayed in the trailer during the week and drove to the next scheduled church on the weekend for the services.

Having gone through the routine of packing our weekend

bags many times, we were well aware of each item we were responsible for grabbing before making our trip. This particular weekend I was to be speaking in Vermont. We had about a five-hour drive ahead of us. As we were throwing our stuff in our satchels, Kathy unthinkingly grabbed the bottle of Pepto Bismol (something she never does). Having packed the van, we set off for the church.

Several hours later, I started getting a bad stomachache. God, in His considerate way, provided the needed solution before the problem arose. Not a life-changing miracle. Simply one more little act of kindness from a God who loves to meet needs.

Another story I could relate might have been a little more serious. We have a two-ton water truck we use to haul the twenty-five hundred gallons of water we use at our live-in facility everyday. One day, I went on a "water run" and stopped at the local lumberyard on the way home. As I stood there talking to the good ole' boy who worked there, he nonchalantly asked, "Is that there yer water truck rollin' across the road?" I ran out to discover the truck sitting across the busy highway, with a line of traffic patiently waiting from each direction. Very sheepishly I jumped in the truck and parked it, grateful that it had not hit anybody.

Another time one of our staff members was driving it and we discovered when he got home that the frame was broken, and there was no reason the several tons of weight sitting on the bed didn't fly off going around one of those Kentucky curves. Both are examples of God's merciful care over our lives.

I noticed these deeds of mercy, but I wonder how many I have missed. When I consider my life before coming to God, all I can think about is how merciful He has been to me. I lived a wild and reckless life. Twelve of my friends were killed during that time. I should have been one of them. Why was I spared? The only explanation is that a good and merciful God knew that the day would come that I would repent. He was carefully watching over my life even before I was one of His.

It was mercy, all mercy—God meeting my needs, just as He has done for you.

Meditation For Today

"Teacher, do You not care that we are perishing?"[1]
The Disciples of Christ

"How long, O LORD, will I call for help, and Thou wilt not hear? I cry out to Thee, 'Violence!' yet Thou dost not save. Why dost Thou make me see iniquity, and cause me to look on wickedness? Yes, destruction and violence are before me; strife exists and contention arises...

"Why dost Thou look with favor on those who deal treacherously? Why art Thou silent when the wicked swallow up those more righteous than they?"[2]
Habakkuk

"And the angel swung his sickle to the earth, and gathered the clusters from the vine of the earth, and threw them into the great wine press of the wrath of God."[3]
The Book of Revelation

Chapter Eight

The Indifference and Anger of God

The "dark side" of God's character is a monumental subject. Volumes have been written about it. One chapter will do it little justice, and yet I feel compelled to touch on this aspect of God; one that creates such confusion in the minds of His followers. How can we call out for mercy from a God who doesn't care, or worse, becomes angry? More importantly, how can we truly surrender to Him? Truthfully, we wouldn't. Our obeisance would be superficial and outward—like that of the aides to the dictator. Without trust there can be no surrender. Without surrender, there can be no victory. It is vital we understand why God does some of the things He does.

The Indifference Of God

Sometimes it is extremely difficult to believe that God cares. Suffering abounds on this ball of dirt called earth. Millions of people starve in Africa—real people, with hopes and dreams similar to yours and mine. Others die of diseases, simply because they can't get medicines we take for granted. Whole villages and cities are brutally exterminated because the people are of a different ethnic background than their killers. Crime runs rampant in our streets as young people turn to drugs in their hopelessness, and parents look on helplessly. Suffering, misery, and unfairness are everywhere we turn. Where is the God of love and mercy in all of this?

Habakkuk struggled with this same issue of suffering and injustice. As he pondered these intimate questions with God in prayer, the Lord showed Habakkuk visions of what was coming to his nation. God described a time of judgment coming to Israel. The marauding armies of Babylonians would destroy everything in Israel. Not exactly a word of encouragement! In the midst of seeing this, Habakkuk spoke the pure Word of God when he stated: "But the righteous will live by his faith." (Habakkuk 2:4)

When nothing makes sense and everything in life seems to be falling apart, Christians have something that sets them apart from the hopelessness of the unsaved: faith in God. God provided reassurance for Habakkuk's doubts. When there is nothing to look forward to but tragedy, only God can give peace.

It was in that frame of mind that Habakkuk said these words that have encouraged believers for thousands of years:

> Though the fig tree should not blossom, and there be no fruit on the vines, though the yield of the olive should fail, and the fields produce no food, though the flock should be cut off from the fold, and there be no cattle in the stalls, yet I will exult in the LORD, I will rejoice in the God of my salvation. The Lord GOD is my strength, and He has made my feet like hinds' feet, and makes me walk on my high places.
> (Habakkuk 3:17-19)

In writing about these verses, Adam Clarke stated:

> These two verses give the finest display of resignation and confidence that I have ever met with. He saw that evil was at hand and unavoidable. He submitted to the dispensation of God whose Spirit enabled him to paint it in all its calamitous circumstances. He knew that God was merciful and gracious.[4]

Matthew Henry wrote:

> He resolves to delight and triumph in God notwithstanding; when all is gone His God is not gone... Those who, when they were full, enjoyed God in all, when they are emptied can enjoy all in God, and can sit down upon a melancholy heap of the ruins and even then sing to the praise and glory of God.[5]

Catherine Marshall, in her excellent book, *Beyond Our Selves*, discusses her own struggles with this as an idealistic young girl. One night, as she was visiting with a godly woman named Mrs. MacDonald, she was able to bring it up.

> On one of these evenings I found myself spilling out my inner rebellion against a God Who permitted suffering and evil when He had the power to stop it.
>
> "Catherine," she said thoughtfully, "you know how often I speak of Kenneth?"
>
> I nodded. Quickly my mind reviewed what I knew about Kenneth. He had been the MacDonalds' only son, had died of diabetes as a teen-ager. It had compounded their sorrow that insulin had been discovered just a few months too late to save their boy. Here then, close at home, was an example of the kind of tragedy that made me question the love of God.
>
> "Well," my friend went on, "if I had reasoned as you suggest, I could have railed bitterly against God for allowing Kenneth's death. God has power. He could have prevented it, so why didn't He?
>
> "Even now, I can't give you a complete answer to that. But I can't be bitter either, because during Kenneth's long illness, I had so many examples of God's tender father-love. Like that time soon after Kenneth himself suspected that he was going to die and asked me, 'Mother, what is it like to die? Mother, does it hurt?'"
>
> Even as Mrs. Mac repeated the questions, tears

sprang to my eyes. "How—did you answer him?"

The white-haired woman seemed to be seeing into the past. "I remember that I fled to the kitchen, supposedly to attend to something on the stove... And I asked God how to answer my boy.

"God did tell me. Only He could have given me the answer to the hardest question that a mother can ever be asked. I knew—just knew how to explain death to him. 'Kenneth,' I remember saying, 'you know how when you were a tiny boy, you used to play so hard all day that when night came, you would be too tired to undress—so you would tumble into Mother's bed and fall asleep?

'"That was not your bed. It was not where you belonged. And you would only stay there a little while. In the morning—to your surprise—you would wake up and find yourself in your own bed in your own room. You were there because someone had loved you and had taken care of you. Your father had come—with his great strong arms—and carried you away.'

"So I told Kenneth that death is like that. We just wake up some morning to find ourselves in another room—our own room, where we belong. We shall be there, because God loves us even more than our human fathers and takes care of us just as tenderly."

We were both silent for a moment. Then Mrs. Mac said softly, "Kenneth never had any fear of dying after that. If—for some reason that I still don't understand—he could not be healed, then this taking away of all fear was the next greatest gift God could give us. And in the end, Kenneth went on into the next life exactly as God had told me he would—gently, sweetly." There was the look of profound peace on my friend's face as she spoke.

After Mrs. Mac tucked me in that night, I lay in the mahogany bed under the eiderdown, pondering her words. What she had really been telling me was that those on the inside of tragedy are often initiated into something that outsiders may not experience at all: the love of God—instant, continuous, real—in the midst of their trouble. With the presence of the Giver, they have something more precious than any gift He might bestow.[6]

Years later, after her husband Peter Marshall died, she found herself answering the same kind of questions to a group of confused teenagers. After the encounter, she reflected on how these questions must affect God.

> Then as I told them of my own gropings toward this answer, I thought of how grieved God must be that any of His children should cower before Him in fright. And I realized how often we attribute emotions and deeds to God that we would ascribe only to the most depraved of human minds. Probably no personality in the universe is so maligned as that of the Creator.[7]

There are some things about this life we simply will not understand until we get to heaven; these must simply be set aside in faith. There are other things, however, that seem evident.

The earth is not meant to be heaven. This is the testing ground of battle; later comes the glory land of reward. It is here in this scene of misery and senseless suffering that we are asked to trust Him. Folks become disenchanted with God because they want Him to make their earthly existence heavenly. We can't know spiritual victory with this immature attitude. This is not heaven. It is not meant to be.

God gives man a free will and won't impose His will upon us. If man wishes to fight wars, conquer kingdoms, and serve Satan, to some extent God must allow him to exercise his free will.

We must understand that in that free will, man hands the title deed of earth over to the devil. Satan has simply done what Satan does. He brings suffering, misery, and destruction to this earth.

We must never forget that we serve a God who suffers with us. He proved this once and for all at Calvary. How can we accuse Him?

God does indeed care about His children and is there for those who call upon Him.

The Anger Of God

The Lord's anger simply cannot be understood in human terms. We get mad when someone offends us, crosses us, or hurts us. Anger is our desire to use force against another person. We feel anger because we are self-centered beings. God has anger, but it is not like ours. His anger is very much a part of His mercy.

Take the story of Saul when he had just been anointed king of Israel. At this point, he was still small in his own eyes. One day, he was out plowing the field when a messenger came with word of a great national threat. Nahash, king of the Ammonites, had besieged the Jewish city of Jabesh-gilead. City leaders offered to surrender to the Ammonites if they would make a covenant with Jabesh-gilead. Nahash responded, "I will make it with you on this condition, that I will gouge out the right eye of every one of you, thus I will make it a reproach on all Israel." (I Samuel 11:2)

The elders asked for a week to send for help and to their astonishment, he agreed. It was one of these messengers who brought Saul word of the incident.

"Then the Spirit of God came upon Saul mightily when he heard these words, and he became very angry." (I Samuel 11:6)

The Spirit of God caused Saul to become angry? The same sweet-natured Spirit we learned about in Chapter Six? Yes, the One and same.

Much of God's anger in the Old Testament is simply a different manifestation of the same consuming fire of love in the New Testament. One day that fire will burn this planet, destroying everything that stands to oppose God or His beloved people. This aspect of His anger is the fiercely protecting love a mother feels for her baby. It is utterly selfless and only thinks about the good of the loved one.

God destroyed the Ammonites, but this utter destruction was an act of mercy. How could that be? The same way it is an act of mercy to society to put an unrepentant murderer to death. The same act by God is judgment to one and mercy to another—depending upon his willingness to repent and submit.

The plagues of Egypt serve as an example. God approached the Egyptians in the only way that captured their attention. Egypt was a powerful nation, accustomed to having things their way. Nobody would turn to God when everything is going his or her way. We turn to Him when we face an overwhelming situation. When we come to the end of our own resources, we respond to the Holy Spirit. God was trying to bring the Egyptians to their knees—so that He could show mercy to them!

Every human has a free will. When God shows up, we can join Him or oppose Him. God came to the Egyptians in a tremendous show of force. He wanted them to humble themselves, repent, and let the Hebrews go. God would have gladly blessed them for it, but these were devil-worshiping people who wanted nothing to do with the God of love. They refused to experience the mercy God extends toward His people. The only alternative to mercy is wrath. They opposed His attempts to free the Hebrews. In the end, it cost them everything. The plagues were acts of mercy to those who joined God and judgment to those who opposed Him.

One problem with our accepting the premise that God is love is that we know so many Old Testament stories dealing with His anger toward wicked nations. It can be hard for us not to see Him as being ready to punish our disobedience when we read such accounts.

Since we can't see things from His perspective, we cannot know how long He had to bear with these wicked groups of people. We are not told everything about His dealings with them, so we don't know to the extremes He went to warning them to save them. We only see the end result: women and children were put to the sword without regard.

Put yourself in God's place for a moment. You try to reveal yourself to mankind. You want men and women to enter into a loving relationship with you, as you already have for them. Groups of people respond differently. Some are very interested. Others are marginal, being in the place where they could be influenced to go either way, while others have no interest and rebuff every attempt you make to reach them.

The uninterested are so given over to wickedness that their lives corrupt others. Modern archaeological evidence reveals a striking example of this. The Canaanites were heavily involved with bestiality. Even children were entirely given over to it! If this weren't bad enough, they worshiped devils—and had sex on the altars as part of their worshipping rites. And if that weren't terrible enough, these people regularly took little babies and threw them onto the white-hot arms of their brass god Molech in the name of religious sacrifice.

All of this is bad enough to warrant their extermination by a holy God, but they were bent on dragging Israel into their cesspool. Jude referred to "the error of Balaam." Balaam was a corrupted prophet of God who showed the Moabites that the way to destroy Israel was by sending beautiful women into their midst and seducing the men into idolatry.

What we do not see from our finite, temporal viewpoints is that the spirit of destruction was continually at work behind the scenes, trying to stamp out God's attempts to reveal Himself through the nation of Israel. The devil understood that if he could corrupt Israel into idolatry (which he managed to do), he could keep hungry hearts from finding God. Satan used those who were wholly given over to worshiping him to corrupt Israel. God, in His wisdom and mercy, knew the only hope was to crush these wicked groups by the hands of the Israelites themselves. Why? So they themselves were fighting the evil that was trying to lure them in.

For context in our lives, we must understand that believers are not saved by how good they are, but by trusting God. It is by grace that we are saved. When we disobey, there are consequences to pay, but consequences for the believer are meant to be a help and a blessing. I thank God for the consequences of my sin that acted like a whip to get me back on the straight and narrow. Without them, I would still be wallowing in the mire of the spiritual pigsty of this world.

You cannot understand God's wrath through the eye of human experience. Our wrath is meant to destroy the one who has offended us. God's wrath is meant in one way or another to bring life. Before you accuse God of being untrustworthy, remember that He laid down His life to save your life. We can't always understand God's dealings with us personally or the world at large, but just the fact that He allowed Himself to be brutally murdered for our sakes should be enough to answer all our doubts.

The Fear of the Lord

   To bring proper balance to our perception of God, we must understand what the Bible refers to when it talks of our need to fear Him. One unfortunate result of our twisted perspective of the Lord's character is a flippant attitude toward Him. Seeing God as just a bigger version of myself causes me to trivialize Him. I feared my father, but not in a way that resulted in a respect for his authority in my life. I feared his temper and his unpredictability. That kind of fear did not produce reverence, but had the opposite effect: I became resentful and rebellious.

   Deep in the human heart lurks an arrogant attitude that we are more fair than God. We lack trust for Him. We have created an entire illusion of what He is like, and it has brought about rebellion toward His authority. Many of us are like the unprofitable servant who refused to obey God saying, "Master, I knew you to be a hard man, reaping where you did not sow, and gathering where you scattered no seed. And I was afraid, and went away and hid your talent in the ground; see, you have what is yours" (Matthew 25:24).

   He knew. There was no question in this man's mind about the nature of his Master. He thought he knew. He thought he had the master all figured out, and somehow what he believed about God relieved him (in his mind) from the necessity of obeying God. The man was hard, so he saw God as being hard. The person who has little concern for others cannot imagine that there are those who do care about people. He believed God was hard because he wanted to believe that way. What we may believe, however, doesn't make it so. One day we will stand before a holy God and see reality. At that moment our staunchly held opinions will be utterly worthless. Many people will stand before a God who tried to reveal Himself, but they were unwilling to listen. Those who did not "have ears to hear" will then hear what the unprofitable servant heard:

   "'You wicked, lazy slave, you knew that I reap where I did not sow, and gather where I scattered no seed. Then you ought to have put my money in the bank, and on my arrival I would have received my money back with interest. Therefore take away the talent from him, and give it to the one who has the ten talents.' For to everyone who has shall more be given, and he shall have an abundance; but from the one who does not have, even what he does have shall be taken away. And cast out the worthless slave into the outer darkness; in that place there shall be weeping and gnashing of teeth" (Matthew 25:26-30).

There is such a thing as a legitimate fear of God. Fear comes from knowledge—correct knowledge. For example, consider the loudmouth who starts smarting off to the little guy standing next to him at the bar, attempting to provoke a fight. Someone leans over and whispers to him that the little guy is the welterweight champion of the world. Suddenly, the correct knowledge serves to put him in his place as he slinks off with his tail between his legs.

I can respect God, not just because He has the power to hurt me, but because, in spite of that power and the fact that I have endlessly provoked Him, He has been kind to me. Jesus said of God, "...He Himself is kind to ungrateful and evil men" (Luke 6:35). As this kindness, in the face of my rebellion and ingratitude, becomes more real to me, a deep reverence begins to form in my heart.

Fear is the sense of being overwhelmed. One aspect of our fear of God comes from being overwhelmed by His kindness, mercy, and love. The deeper the revelation of God, the deeper the sense of being overwhelmed by His goodness. It is in the light of this understanding that we see the words reverence and awe as accurate synonyms for fear.

Another thing that creates fear of God is the realization that it is only His grace that keeps us from falling back into the pit He pulled us out of. The Lord gave a former homosexual man who went through our live-in program a deep revelation of this. He had been complaining in his prayer time about his lack of fear for God. Just then the Lord spoke to him: *You don't fear Me? Then why don't you go back into your sin?* As the Lord spoke those words to my friend, the reality of the homosexual lifestyle came rushing in on him. In an instant, he vividly remembered the emptiness, the misery, and the degrading things he once did. It came to his mind in a flood and all he could do was to thank the Lord for saving him out of that hell. To my friend Winston, fearing the Lord means fearing the loss of His grace that keeps us from our sin. It means fearing a separation from Him and being left to oneself.

The man who really knows God fears being separated from Him. He might struggle with tempting thoughts about things he has done in the past, but the thought of returning to that old way of life strikes dread in his heart. That man knows only too well what life without God is like. Despite the alluring temptations, the thought of life outside God's presence is frightening.

The vague notion of dying and going to a place with a lot of fire is not enough to persuade people to obey God. It may help them to make the initial commitment, but eventually there must be a stronger conviction to keep them on the "straight and narrow." For the man who has enjoyed the love of God and has seen the emptiness of sin, the thought of life without God is enough to keep him.

Personally, much of my fear of God comes from His dealings with me. The Lord has dealt with me very severely. One of the most precious experiences of my life was when He crushed me at that altar call I referred to earlier. I ran into God that day and in one instant, was transformed into a blubbering baby. After that experience, I had a new-found respect for Him. In fact, I feared Him. Those who have never been broken by God usually have little fear of Him.

A friend of mine says: "I love being in that place of brokenness with God. It's what I have to experience to get there that scares me! It's better to try to stay humble than to have to go through what it takes to be humbled." Being disciplined by the Lord is not fun. The man who goes through God's chastisement learns to fear it. The fear of the rod tends to keep the sheep in line.

The reality of what awaits us at judgment also brings us into this attitude of fear. Paul said, "each man's work will become evident" in that day" (I Corinthians 3:13). Jesus said, "whatever you have said in the dark shall be heard in the light, and what you have whispered in the inner rooms shall be proclaimed upon the housetops" (Luke 12:3). Think about the reality of these two statements. We will one day stand before the Lord where our deeds and words will be judged (this is not the Great White Throne judgment for the lost). It seems as though everything we have done—along with the real motivation behind it—will be shown for all in heaven to see. How terrifying to think that all my petty selfishness and pride will be exposed to all!*

We should also fear being judged by the same measure with which we have judged others. I realize well-meaning teachers have so explained away the words of Jesus that they no longer seem to carry any threat. This watering down of Jesus' words is part of the reason we lack fear of God. Jesus said these words and I believe He meant exactly what He said: "Do not judge lest you be judged. For in the way you judge, you will be judged; and by your standard of measure, it will be measured to you" (Matthew 7:1-2).

I will only make a passing reference to this passage now as I will deal with it more fully later. I think it could help us to take a moment to reflect upon the standard of measurement we have measured out to others. Some of us judge everybody who comes across our path. From our self-centered perspective, we do everything right and everybody will be judged according to how they treat us or satisfy our requirements. In our self-exalted minds, we become like a movie critic, examining the lives of all we have contact with. How frightful the thought that those who think this way will be judged in the same lack of mercy!

Believers need not ever fear God in the way a cowering child fears her drunken father, or in the way a petty official fears the murderous dictator he serves. God is loving, consistent, and absolutely just. We needn't be concerned with Him getting mad at us.

It is true, however, that many of us are too flippant with this holy God. Not only does He deserve better, but there will be an accounting for each of us one day. When the truth of our lives is shown on the giant screen in heaven, what we will see is a loving God who multiplied mercies to us by the thousands—if not millions. None of us will be able to accuse Him of being a hard taskmaster. Instead, that screen will show our own unwillingness to reciprocate that love to the Lord and to give out the mercy to those around us that

---

*My personal opinion on these verses is that those attitudes and habits of life of which we have repented will be done away with. There will be no reason to bring them up. I tend to think these verses refer to areas in our lives that we wouldn't consecrate to Him. We will need to see why we lost rewards where rewards could have been won.

He has lavished on us.

Angry and indifferent? Not at all. To be feared? With everything within us!

Meditation For Today

"O LORD, Thou hast searched me and known me. Thou dost know when I sit down and when I rise up; Thou dost understand my thought from afar. Thou dost scrutinize my path and my lying down, and art intimately acquainted with all my ways. Even before there is a word on my tongue, behold, O LORD, Thou dost know it all. Thou hast enclosed me behind and before, and laid Thy hand upon me. Such knowledge is too wonderful for me; it is too high, I cannot attain to it.

Where can I go from Thy Spirit? Or where can I flee from Thy presence? If I ascend to heaven, Thou art there; if I make my bed in Sheol, behold, Thou art there. If I take the wings of the dawn, if I dwell in the remotest part of the sea, even there Thy hand will lead me, and Thy right hand will lay hold of me...

For Thou didst form my inward parts; Thou didst weave me in my mother's womb. I will give thanks to Thee, for I am fearfully and wonderfully made; wonderful are Thy works, and my soul knows it very well. My frame was not hidden from Thee, when I was made in secret, and skillfully wrought in the depths of the earth. Thine eyes have seen my unformed substance; and in Thy book they were all written, the days that were ordained for me, when as yet there was not one of them. How precious also are Thy thoughts to me, O God! How vast is the sum of them! If I should count them, they would outnumber the sand. When I awake, I am still with Thee...

Search me, O God, and know my heart; try me and know my anxious thoughts; and see if there be any hurtful way in me, and lead me in the everlasting way."[1]

David

Chapter Nine

The God Who Works

In 1978, the Israeli intelligence agency, Mossad, discovered that France had agreed to supply Iraq with 150 pounds of 93-percent-enriched uranium to be used in a 700-megawatt commercial nuclear reactor which France would help build. Ostensibly, this was to be used for peaceful purposes, primarily providing energy for Baghdad. The Israelis suspected Iraqi strongman Saddam Hussein had other ideas.

Operation Sphinx was immediately launched and given top priority within the clandestine halls of Mossad headquarters. Eight separate teams of intelligence specialists were assigned to the case. After an initial review of the available information, they chose an Iraqi scientist named Halim as their target. Halim and his wife lived in Paris while working on the project in a French laboratory.

The world famous spy organization quickly went to work. First, a group of operations agents was sent to Paris. Their task was to act as support staff for the other agents involved in the undertaking. Arriving in Paris on different flights and at different times, they immediately went to work securing "safe houses," different dwellings which housed the more than 50 agents who resided in Paris during the operation. Food, supplies, furniture and many other details were supplied and maintained so that the principle agents could focus on the job at hand. Special offices and a penthouse suite were rented as well.

Once lodging was secured, the field supervisors arrived on the scene. Their job was to oversee the entire project, to manage the various agents, coordinate events, and make plans and decisions each step of the way.

Next the surveillance crews showed up. Their primary duty was to watch Halim and his wife to determine where they went, their daily activities, and their associations to gather as much information about them as possible. This covert undertaking required meticulous execution—there was no room for error. Different teams of agents were assigned to follow them throughout the day—man painting a house down the street, a couple who had just moved into a house nearby, several agents in a revolving series of vehicles followed their travels. Had the couple detected any such activity, the entire operation would have failed.

A separate crew of specialists was brought in for electronic surveillance. Their task was to break into Halim's home and plant bugs in different rooms of the house and the telephone. Once this was accomplished, people listened to everything going on in the home 24 hours a day. These listeners had to be Israelis who were familiar with the Iraqi dialect of the Arabic language. Each day, each surveillance crew reported its findings to the field supervisors.

And finally, when everything else was in place, the primary contact team arrived to begin their phase of the operation. These were the people who had direct contact with Halim and his wife. An assortment of men and women of various nationalities played different parts in this elaborate scheme with one purpose in mind: to get Halim to willingly give the Israelis information about the nuclear complex being built in the heart of Iraq.

Once everybody was in place, the supervisors held a meeting with the crew leaders of each team. The visual surveillance agents reported that the only thing Halim did regularly was catch a bus down the street from his house everyday. The electronic surveillance team overheard two vital pieces of information which they brought to the meeting. After listening to countless hours of casual conversation, one heated discussion gave them important data for the operation. It came after a beautiful Israeli spy, posing as a French student, showed up at the front door. "I saw how you looked at that girl," Samira told her husband. "Don't you get any ideas just because I'm going away. I know what you are." Through that one statement they ascertained that his wife was leaving and that he apparently had a history of adultery. After compiling all of the available data, the plan was developed. A former agent tells what happened next:

> Butrus Eben Halim could be forgiven for noticing the woman. After all, she was a sultry blonde, given to wearing tight pants and low-cut blouses, revealing just enough of herself to pique any man's desire for more.
>
> She'd been showing up at his regular bus stop in Villejuif on the southern outskirts of Paris every day for the past week. With just two buses using that stop—one local and one RATP into Paris—and usually only a few other passengers standing around, it was impossible to miss her. Although Halim didn't know it, that was the point.
>
> It was August 1978. Her routine, like his, seemed constant. She was there when Halim arrived to catch his bus. Moments later, a light-skinned, blue-eyed, sharply dressed man would race up in a red Ferrari BB512 two-seater, pull in to pick up the blonde, then speed off to heaven knew where...
>
> One day, the second bus arrived before the Ferrari. The woman first glanced down the street searching for the car, then shrugged and boarded the bus. Halim's bus had been temporarily delayed by a minor "accident" two blocks away when a Peugeot pulled out in front of it.
>
> Moments later, the Ferrari arrived. The driver looked around for the girl, and Halim, realizing what had happened, shouted to him in French that she had taken the bus. The man, looking perplexed, replied in English, at which point Halim repeated the story for him in English.
>
> Grateful, the man asked Halim where he was

headed. Halim told him the Madeleine station, within walking distance of Saint-Lazare, and the driver, Ran. S.—whom Halim would know only as Englishman Jack Donovan—said he, too, was heading that way, and offered him a lift.

Why not, Halim thought, hopping into the car and settling in for the drive.

The fish had swallowed the hook. And as luck would have it, it would prove to be a prize catch for the Mossad.[2]

Over the next several weeks, Donovan developed a relationship with Halim. One day he convinced Halim to join him on an overnight business trip to another French city. It supposedly involved a deal where he would buy cargo containers from a businessman and then sell them to some African country to use as housing units. As Donovan and the "businessman" haggled over the price, the crane picked up one of the containers. Halim noticed, as it was planned for him to do, that the bottom of the container was rusted. He quickly took Donovan aside and told him about it. Donovan, using this piece of helpful information, was able to negotiate a better price with the "businessman." Donovan gave Halim $1,000 for his help. The second hook was now in place.

Little by little, over several weeks, using hookers and money as lures, Halim was getting deeper and deeper involved. Finally, the agents were ready to go in for the kill.

Two days later, Donovan returned and called Halim. Over coffee, Halim could plainly see that his friend was upset about something.

"I've got the chance of a superb deal from a German company on some special pneumatic tubes for shipping radioactive material for medical purposes," said Donovan. "It's all very technical. There's big money involved, but I don't know the first thing about it. They've put me on to an English scientist who's agreed to inspect the tubes. The problem is he wants too much money and I'm not sure I trust him, in any case. I think he's tied in with the Germans."

"Maybe I could help," said Halim.

"Thanks, but I need a scientist to examine these tubes."

"I am a scientist," said Halim.

Donovan, looking surprised, said, "What do you mean? I thought you were a student."

"I had to tell you that at first. But I'm a scientist sent here by Iraq on a special project. I'm sure I could help."...

"Listen, I'm supposed to meet this lot in Amsterdam this weekend. I must go a day or two early, but how be if I send my jet for you on Saturday morning?"

Halim agreed.

"You won't regret this," said Donovan. "There's a packet of money to be made if these things are legitimate."

The jet, temporarily painted with Donovan's company logo, was a Learjet flown in from Israel for the occasion. The Amsterdam office belonged to a wealthy Jewish contractor...

When Halim arrived at the Amsterdam office in the limousine that met him at the airport, the others were already there. The two businessmen were Itsik E., a Mossad katsa, and Benjamin Goldstein, an Israeli nuclear scientist carrying a German passport. He'd brought along one of the pneumatic tubes as the display model for Halim to examine.

After some initial discussions, Ran and Itsik left the room, supposedly to work out the financial details, leaving the two scientists together to discuss technical matters. With their common interest and expertise, the two men sensed an instant camaraderie and Goldstein asked Halim how he knew so much about the nuclear industry. It was a shot in the dark, but Halim, his defenses dropped completely, told him about his job.

Later, when Goldstein told Itsik about Halim's admission, they decided to take the unsuspecting Iraqi to dinner. Ran was to make an excuse for being unable to attend.

Over dinner, the two men outlined a plan they said they had been working on: trying to sell nuclear power plants to Third World countries—for peaceful purposes, of course.

"Your plant project would make a perfect model for us to sell to these people," said Itsik. "If you could just get us some details, the plans, that sort of thing, we would all stand to make a fortune from this."...

"And isn't it, well, you know, kind of dangerous?"

"No. There's no danger," said Itsik. "You must have regular access to these things. We just want to use it as a model, that's all. We'd pay you well and nobody would ever know. How could they? This sort of thing is done all the time."

"I suppose so," said Halim, still hesitating, but intrigued by the prospect of big money...

Now they really had him. The promise of untold riches was just too much. Anyway, he felt good about Goldstein, and it wasn't as if he was helping them design a bomb. And there was no need for Donovan to ever know. So why not? he thought.

Halim had been officially recruited. And like so many recruits, he wasn't even aware of it.[3]

In 1981, thanks to the information given to them by Halim, the Israeli air force was able to pinpoint their bombs on the reactor located within the Iraqi power plant, thereby destroying Saddam Hussein's ability to produce nuclear weapons. All of their efforts were richly rewarded.

The story of the Mossad's operation may seem a bit out of place in a book about spiritual victory. But the immense effort put into that operation by dozens of specialists, all focused on the life of one man with the purpose of manipulating the events of his life to cause him to make the decision they wanted him to make, is an excellent illustration of the enormity of God's involvement in the lives of His children.

Earlier, you read that one of the reasons people have a difficult time believing in the goodness of God is that they often don't recognize it in their lives. People tend to chalk things up to fate or to what Hannah Whitall Smith calls, "second causes," meaning other people. But she, like every other believer who has gone to any depth into the knowledge of God, sees His sovereign hand in everything that comes into life.

> Second causes must all be under the control of our Father. Not one of them can touch us except with His knowledge and by His permission. No man or company of men, no power in earth or heaven, can touch that soul which is abiding in Christ without first passing through His encircling presence and receiving the seal of His permission.[4]

I remember a conversation I had with my late friend, Nelson Hinman, in my early days of ministry. Nels was nearly 80 and he and his wife, Juanita, had been a tremendous help to Kathy and me as we began Pure Life Ministries. I was grappling with many things that day. How much power does the devil have? What part does spiritual warfare play in our ministries? How can I make Pure Life Ministries a success? How do I get more help from God? What about those who oppose and hinder me?

I didn't know it at the time, but I was struggling with an age-old question about God's involvement in the believer's life. Nels listened quietly that day, not quick to give advice. Finally, as I sat there like a school kid waiting for the teacher's wisdom, he spoke. "Steve," he said, straightening up in his easy chair, "all I can tell you is that the longer I serve God, the more I realize His sovereignty in my life." I knew that was all he was going to say about the subject and I took it to heart.

From that day on I began realizing how much God is at work in my daily life. The more I saw my Father's care, the smaller the devil looked. I began seeing many of my setbacks in ministry as the

Lord's loving discipline and care over my life. Troublesome people were sent to help me deal with flaws in my own nature. Through this unfolding revelation came a much needed rest of soul for me: "If the Lord loves me and is in control of the circumstances of my life, I simply need not fear nor worry."

This was the point Jesus made in that celebrated portion of the Sermon on the Mount. I realize many of you know this; nevertheless, I invite you to take a few minutes with this section of Scripture and allow these words to penetrate your heart:

> For this reason I say to you, do not be anxious for your life, as to what you shall eat, or what you shall drink; nor for your body, as to what you shall put on. Is not life more than food, and the body than clothing? Look at the birds of the air, that they do not sow, neither do they reap, nor gather into barns, and yet your heavenly Father feeds them. Are you not worth much more than they? And which of you by being anxious can add a single cubit to his life's span?
>
> And why are you anxious about clothing? Observe how the lilies of the field grow; they do not toil nor do they spin, yet I say to you that even Solomon in all his glory did not clothe himself like one of these. But if God so arrays the grass of the field, which is alive today and tomorrow is thrown into the furnace, will He not much more do so for you, O men of little faith? Do not be anxious then, saying, "What shall we eat?" or "What shall we drink?" or "With what shall we clothe ourselves?"
>
> For all these things the Gentiles eagerly seek; for your heavenly Father knows that you need all these things. But seek first His kingdom and His righteousness; and all these things shall be added to you. Therefore do not be anxious for tomorrow; for tomorrow will care for itself. Each day has enough trouble of its own. (Matthew 6:25-34).

Jesus was in perfect peace because He knew the reality of life:

His Heavenly Father, who maintains the entire universe, can be trusted to keep our lives and souls. We need not strain to make things happen or to protect ourselves. Our Father knows exactly what we need.

God's Enormous Investment In The Life Of A Believer

The fact of the matter is that God has been deeply involved with your life since your birth. You have been the focus of an immense heavenly operation for many years. Who can know the number of angels assigned at various times to watch over you? Who can guess how many people God has used in a myriad of ways to influence and mold your life, to bring you to the point of seeing your great need for Him? How many different circumstances of your life—loss, failures, problems, difficult people—did God use to bring you to that momentous decision? Paul rightly said, "You were bought with a price..." Of course the greatest price paid was on Calvary, but how much else has gone into our salvation?

Unquestionably, God has been intricately involved in the life of every single person who comes to Him; however, coming to God is only the beginning. At this point, the real work begins. Paul said, "And we know that God causes all things to work together for good to those who love God, to those who are called according to His purpose. For whom He foreknew, He also predestined to become conformed to the image of His Son, that He might be the first-born among many brethren" (Romans 8:28-29).

Once God has helped a man come to repentance, the next phase of the operation begins. By utilizing various circumstances that tend to nudge the believer in the right direction—godly teaching and counsel, the lives of mature saints, the conviction of sin, the passion for holiness He plants in the heart, and a host of other elements perfectly tailored for that person's situation—the Lord is constantly trying to do a work in the believer's life. Such tireless effort is aimed at making him more like Jesus. It is, if you will, a major Mossad operation going on at all times around a Christian's daily routine. Just like Halim, most people are completely oblivious to all of this activity.

God's Tremendous Care And Concern

One of my wife's most endearing characteristics is her insisting to be involved with me constantly. For instance, when I wake up in the middle of the night (I am a chronic insomniac), her eyes immediately pop open to see what I'm doing. Usually she's such a good sleeper that she could easily sleep right through the night. And yet, somehow, she always knows when I wake up. She says she can hear my eyelids open! If I get out of bed to read or do something to avoid bothering her, she insists on me staying there, even though turning the light on means she will lose sleep. My wife wants to be involved with everything that goes on with me. It isn't out of nosiness or out of being insecure about my faithfulness. She simply loves me and is absorbed in every phase of my life. To Kathy, love equates with undying interest.

So it is with God. He has a tremendous investment in every believer's life and is greatly interested in every aspect of it. He loves His children and it is the joy of His great heart to be involved with the details of their lives. The Psalmist certainly understood this: "Behold, the eye of the LORD is on those who fear Him, on those who hope for His lovingkindness" (Psalm 33:18). So did David, who said, "How precious also are Thy thoughts to me, O God! How vast is the sum of them! If I should count them, they would outnumber the sand..." (Psalm 139:17-18).

God is intimately and intricately involved in the lives of His people. He is constantly at work in every aspect of their lives. But everything He does is for a purpose. Like the massive and complicated Mossad operation, God is quietly working behind the scenes of our daily lives with a purpose in mind which is of extreme importance to Him.

The Great Work Of God

God's greatest works aren't the majestic Himalaya mountains, the intricate, tropical beauties of Hawaii, or the brilliant colors found in the deepest sea. They aren't the plagues of Egypt, the parting of the Red Sea, or David's killing of Goliath. His greatest works certainly aren't someone shaking on the floor after receiving prayer. These are all comparatively simple deeds for the One who spoke the universe into being.

His most fabulous work on earth is displayed when He transforms a person who is self-centered, full of pride, and has very little concern for other people, into someone who is so full of Jesus and His love that he continually, in his daily life, puts the will of God and the needs of others before his own desires. Nothing is greater than when God turns a loser into a winner!

David said, "For Thou didst form my inward parts... wonderful are Thy works..." (Psalm 139:13-14). Inward parts is a Hebraic expression, *kilyah*, referring to a person's inside world, or inner self. God is constantly at work in the lives of those who love Him.

Paul said, "Therefore, if anyone is in Christ, he is a new creation; the old has gone, the new has come!" (II Corinthians 5:17 NIV). He also said, "For we are God's workmanship, created in Christ Jesus to do good works, which God prepared in advance for us to do" (Ephesians 2:10). Zechariah said that God forms the spirit of the man within him (Zechariah 12:1). While the Psalmist said, "He who fashions the hearts of them all, He who understands all their works" (Psalms 33:15). These verses describe a God who is at work forming something beautiful within a person.

In Jeremiah 18, we find the prophet illustrating this truth with the concept of the potter and the clay. W.F. Adeney, one of the expositors of *The Pulpit Commentary,* brings out the richness of God's sovereign work in the lives of His people.

> But on closer consideration, while it teaches lessons of humility and reverent submission on our part, it also throws light on the merciful goodness of God, and encourages us both to hope and to act for that which will lead to our highest blessedness.
> I. Men are under the absolute power of God, like clay in the hands of the potter... God has also absolute authority over us. He has the ultimate right of supreme sovereignty to do as he will with his subjects. Yet there is nothing alarming in this fact, but rather an infinite consolation. For God is not a heartless, conscienceless despot, displaying arbitrary power by mere caprice; he is holy, and exercises his sovereignty according to principles of strict justice, truth, and right. He is gracious, and rules with purposes of love for the good of his creatures...

II. Men can no more attain a worthy end in life without God than the clay can become a shapely vessel without the potter. There lies the clay—a dead, heavy, amorphous mass, with no possibility of spontaneously generating forms of beauty, with no secret principle of evolution to work it into something orderly. We are as clay. Except God wrought in us and upon us, we could simply lie helpless, only to waste away with the flux of circumstances...

III. God has a purpose in every life as the potter has with the clay. There is a meaning for the strange discipline of providence. God is shaping us into that form which he deems most fitting. Every life has not the same purpose. The potter makes vessels of innumerable shapes. Yet each life is successful as its own particular purpose is fulfilled. The homely jug may be perfect, though it is very different from the graceful vase...

IV. God shapes our lives by the discipline of providence as the potter the clay upon his wheels. The wheel of time spins fast, but not carrying us away, changing but not destroying each separate individuality. In providence there are wheels within wheels. We do not understand their meaning. The clay is pressed now below into a solid base, now above into a dainty rim, but it is difficult to see what the final outcome will be till all is finished. So our lives are pressed on one side and on another—something which in our eyes is indispensable is taken away, something which to us seems needless is added. But out of the dizzy whirl, the rush and confusion of life, God is steadily working out his purpose.

V. God will ultimately accomplish his purpose in us, though at first it seems to fail. The clay is refractory. It must be broken up and remodeled. Man is more than clay. He has free-will, mysterious as may be the connection of this with the almighty sovereignty of God. In a much more terrible way he too is refractory, willfully and stubbornly. For this he must be broken. His life must be disturbed and shaken up, but only that God may begin again to fashion him for his destined end. Great disappointments, destructive events, the failure of a man's work, the disruption of a Church, the revolution of a nation, may seem simply disastrous. But we see how that by means of these things God, in his infinite patience and gracious perseverance, will finally effect his own great purposes, and so secure the true blessedness of his creatures.[5]

God's Balancing Act

Unlike the Mossad, the Lord's involvement in our lives is by no means to hurt, use, or abuse us. When you care about someone, you are careful about how you treat them. The believer isn't someone to be manipulated into doing what God wants, and then to be thrown away like the Mossad did with Halim. All of the Lord's efforts are motivated by His immense love for that person.

To properly work in a man's life, the Lord takes extensive care over everything He does. Too much scolding can crush a man's spirit. Likewise, excessive leniency could allow him to wander off into unspeakable perils. Not only must the Lord concern himself with a man's life, He also considers how His workings are going to affect those He is using or those who interact with the subject of His great care.

Years ago I was scheduled to preach at a certain church for both Sunday services. The pastor inadvertently double-booked that Sunday. Forgetting that he had invited me to speak, he also asked a denominational dignitary to speak that Sunday. He resolved the problem by having me speak in the morning service, while the other minister was to speak in the evening service. That meant that this elderly minister, who held a very prominent position in his denomination, would be in attendance when I spoke that morning.

As it turns out, God really moved. I could feel His presence as I preached and a fire in my words that day pierced every heart. During the altar call, the visiting minister who sat on the front row, practically dove out of the pew onto the altar, crying out to God in heart-felt repentance. Later, he came to me privately and told me that my words had really affected him.

I left that city the next day buoyant. It was a real honor to be used in this man's life in that way. But underneath it all, there was also an ugly splotch of pride growing inside my heart. It wasn't anything massive, but it was there nonetheless.

The following week I had to speak at a large church in another state. Kathy and I arrived that Sunday morning in time for the staff prayer time. Overhearing one godly woman fervently praying for the meeting and on the heels of what had happened the week before, I felt as though God was going to move in a mighty way that morning. I said to the pastor, "I have a strong word for this church this morning. I think God is going to do something."

Later, when he introduced me to the congregation, he told them that I had said that I had a *powerful* word for them that morning. Even though I engaged in secret pride during the previous week, I knew better than to make a statement like that! I should have seen the handwriting on the wall. God was setting me up!

As I started into my message that morning, the wireless microphone began cutting out. Just as I was getting to the place of making a strong point, the soundman had to come up to the pulpit and fiddle with the mike for a few minutes while I just stood there. I got started again, but after that, I just felt flat inside. I didn't sense the Lord's presence at all. My words seemed weak. Sure enough, when I gave the altar call, only a handful of people came forward. What a major disappointment!

Someone later told me, "Oh, that's the devil, brother. He was trying to stop what God wanted to do." I knew better than that. I found out later that there were reasons for the lack of response, but God was also using this experience to mold my character.

He would, no doubt, love to use me as He had in the first church more often. But as soon as He begins moving powerfully like that, I start puffing up with secret pride, feeling as though He can use me that way because of how godly I am. Then He has to humble me. But He can't humble me too much because I'm so sensitive that I can't take too much correction at one time without going into a dump! He has to temper His discipline so that I won't be overwhelmed by it.

Because God takes an all-inclusive approach in meeting the

needs of others, He wanted to use me in order to affect the pastor and his congregation. The next week, knowing He needed to humble me, He did it in such a way to avoid detrimentally affecting the others of that congregation.

God is constantly involved in all of our lives, and in His involvement, He has to continually balance everything He does.

Part of the life of victory comes about when the believer can rest in the assurance that God truly loves him, is looking to help him, and is extremely involved in his life. He can make that deep surrender because the Lord has successfully proven His trustworthiness.

The next step toward real victory comes as the believer begins to appropriate the divine mercy that is his for the taking. This brings us back to where we began: seeing our need for His help.

Part Three
Turning God's Mercy
Into Your Victory

Meditation For Today

"One of the greatest revelations is that Jesus does not appear to a man because he deserves it, but out of the generosity of His own heart on the ground of the man's need. Let me recognize I need Him, and He will appear... The more complete our sense of need, the more satisfactory is our dependence on God... God loves the man who needs Him."[1]

Oswald Chambers

"I have been driven many times to my knees by the overwhelming conviction that I had nowhere else to go."[2]

Abraham Lincoln

"Prayer is not overcoming God's reluctance; it is laying hold of his highest willingness."[3]

Richard Chenevix Trench

"For we do not have a high priest who cannot sympathize with our weaknesses, but One who has been tempted in all things as we are, yet without sin. Let us therefore draw near with confidence to the throne of grace, that we may receive mercy and may find grace to help in time of need."[4]

The Book of Hebrews

Chapter Ten

The Cry of the Needy

One word describes the human being: NEED.

As humans, we require oxygen to breath, but it cannot just be pure oxygen, it must also contain the proper mixture of nitrogen. Humans need water to drink; we cannot exist more than a few days without it. We need food to eat, but it must contain all of the many nutrients our bodies need to function. We need blood flowing through our veins, and we will expire if the quantity becomes too low. Human beings must be kept warm lest we die from some cold-related disease; we cannot become too warm, or we will die of heat exhaustion. We must not only be kept warm, but we must be kept dry, or we will die of hypothermia. And lastly, we need light to see, lest we find it impossible to provide ourselves with all of our other needs.

To provide for all of these needs, God created a world just the right distance from the sun, with just the right combination of gases in the atmosphere, with animal and plant life to provide food and nutrients, and with materials to make clothes and shelters.

Surely the Psalmist was right when he said, "The earth is full of the lovingkindness of the LORD" (Psalms 33:5). Yes, this earth was supplied for all of our needs. However, our needs are not confined to the realm of nature. We have a need greater than that of sustaining physical life: it is spiritual life.

God, in the infinite depths of His wisdom, created a three-dimensional world that people could see, hear, and touch. In this world, He supplied everything for our basic physical needs. There is one thing about this world, though, that many do not realize: it lies outside of the dimension that He exists in.

As things are, a person can live a full life on earth without ever once showing any concern or interest in this unseen realm. If his physical needs are being met, he may never feel compelled to look outside of the comfortable domain of his daily life. If calamity or great adversity comes his way, he often makes a quick search for a Greater Power to help him.

This is God's great moment. He sometimes works with a person for 20, 30, or even 60 years to prepare him for the moment when he is ready to halt his forward movement through life to explore the possibility that maybe he missed something on the way.

In some ways God created man to be self-sufficient in this world. In other ways He made him to need something that only He can supply. The Lord often puts a person into some situation so that he can see his need and cry out to God for help. The blinding effects of pride and rebellion keep the person from doing it.

For some people, God must work very carefully around their fragile (and often monstrous) egos to bring them to the point where they will look outside of themselves to seek Him. It is a tribute to the great longsuffering nature of God that He is willing to go through such pains to save a man's soul.* But God is willing because this is what God lives for. He works tirelessly for years and years to bring people to the point of seeing their need. When it happens, a tremendous celebration breaks forth in God's domain. Jesus said, "I tell you that in the same way, there will be more joy in heaven over one sinner who repents, than over ninety-nine righteous persons who need no repentance" (Luke 15:7). Imagine that—joy in heaven! Over what? Someone sees his impoverished condition and cries out to God in repentance.

---

* What a shame we are so unappreciative of all that God has done to get us to that point! How shameful it is that we fight and resist Him as He attempts to keep us in sight of our need!

Drawn To Need

If one thing is clear in Scripture, it is God's propensity toward and affinity for the afflicted, poor, downtrodden, and needy of this world. Hannah exulted, "The LORD makes poor and rich; He brings low, He also exalts. He raises the poor from the dust, He lifts the needy from the ash heap to make them sit with nobles..." (I Samuel 2:8).

David said, "The humble have seen it and are glad; you who seek God, let your heart revive. For the LORD hears the needy, and does not despise His who are prisoners" (Psalms 69:33).

His son Solomon wrote, "For he will deliver the needy when he cries for help, the afflicted also, and him who has no helper. He will have compassion on the poor and needy, and the lives of the needy he will save. He will rescue their life from oppression and violence; and their blood will be precious in his sight;" (Psalms 72:12-14).

The Psalmist stated, "But He sets the needy securely on high away from affliction... Who is wise? Let him give heed to these things; and consider the lovingkindnesses of the LORD" (Psalms 107:41).

Isaiah declared to the Lord, "For Thou hast been a defense for the helpless, a defense for the needy in his distress, a refuge from the storm, a shade from the heat; for the breath of the ruthless is like a rain storm against a wall" (Isaiah 25:4).

And finally the Lord Himself revealed His heart toward those in need: "'Because of the devastation of the afflicted, because of the groaning of the needy, now I will arise,' says the LORD; I will set him in the safety for which he longs'" (Psalms 12:5).

God is irresistibly drawn to the needy and when we cry out for His help, we are putting ourselves into the enviable position of receiving from God. He has an unstoppable compulsion to help those who ask for help. While God favors the poor and desires to help them whenever He can, people must cry out to Him for help before He is able to respond. * It may be nothing more than a quiet peep deep within someone's heart but is heard clearly in the throne room of God.

---

* Hell is full of people who were poor in this life but refused to repent. However, you can see the Lord's heart for their plight on earth through the provisions for the poor in the Law and through the countless believers down through the centuries to help the downtrodden.

Instructing His disciples how to pray, Jesus used these two stories:

> Now He was telling them a parable to show that at all times they ought to pray and not to lose heart, saying, "There was in a certain city a judge who did not fear God, and did not respect man. And there was a widow in that city, and she kept coming to him, saying, 'Give me legal protection from my opponent.' And for a while he was unwilling; but afterward he said to himself, 'Even though I do not fear God nor respect man, yet because this widow bothers me, I will give her legal protection, lest by continually coming she wear me out.'" And the Lord said, "Hear what the unrighteous judge said; now shall not God bring about justice for His elect, who cry to Him day and night, and will He delay long over them?" (Luke 18:1-7).
>
> And He said to them, "Suppose one of you shall have a friend, and shall go to him at midnight, and say to him, 'Friend, lend me three loaves; for a friend of mine has come to me from a journey, and I have nothing to set before him'; and from inside he shall answer and say, 'Do not bother me; the door has already been shut and my children and I are in bed; I cannot get up and give you anything.' I tell you, even though he will not get up and give him anything because he is his friend, yet because of his persistence he will get up and give him as much as he needs" (Luke 11:5-8).

Both stories show us the way the kingdom of heaven works. God responds to persistent, heart-felt cries for help.

Crying Out For Victory

In *At The Altar Of Sexual Idolatry*, I wrote the following to sexual addicts who have made countless trips to the altar but have come away feeling hopeless:

> No one understands to the fullest all that is

involved in answered prayer or being set free from bondage. However, we do know that the Lord has given us important principles here that we can depend on to help us. If you doubt that God really listens to the cries of His children, examine these passages that boast of His mercy:

Then we cried to the LORD, the God of our fathers, and the LORD heard our voice and saw our affliction and our toil and our oppression; and the LORD brought us out of Egypt with a mighty hand and an outstretched arm and with great terror and with signs and wonders. (Deuteronomy 26:7-8)

And when the sons of Israel cried to the LORD, the LORD raised up a deliverer for the sons of Israel to deliver them, Othniel the son of Kenaz, Caleb's younger brother. (Judges 3:9)

But when the sons of Israel cried to the LORD, the LORD raised up a deliverer for them, Ehud the son of Gera, the Benjamite, a left-handed man... (Judges 3:15)

And the sons of Israel cried to the LORD... And the LORD routed Sisera and all his chariots and all his army, with the edge of the sword before Barak; and Sisera alighted from his chariot and fled away on foot. (Judges 4:3, 15)

Now it came about when the sons of Israel cried to the LORD on account of Midian, that the LORD sent a prophet to the sons of Israel... (Judges 6:7-8)

These passages are just a few accounts of God's response to the cries of His people. Time and time again the nation of Israel would get themselves into trouble because of their disobedience. Yet, whenever they cried out to God for His help, He would rescue them. Your situation might be much the same as that of Israel. It is because of your disobedience that you are in the predicament you find yourself in, and yet there is a merciful God who hears the cries of His children.

I once thought that all of the trips I made to the altar crying out for God's help were a waste of time. Then as I re-examined those isolated incidents, I came to realize that those trips to the altar were instrumental in bringing about my deliverance! If you really want to be set free from the bondage of sexual sin, cry out to God daily. Do it today! Do it now! Your cries will be heard![5]

Having Faith For Victory

One major obstacle that hinders us from receiving from God is unbelief. The typical American Christian who goes to church, listens to radio preachers, and reads their books would probably be mortified to realize how much unbelief pervades his heart. Most believers assume they are full of faith, thinking this way because their faith has been largely untested. We do not suffer the persecution, deprivation, or calamity that many of our brothers and sisters around the world do. We are "fair weather friends" until proven otherwise. Many of us trust ourselves 24 hours a day, seven days a week, until something comes up that we cannot handle, and then we call on the Lord. We wonder why He does not move heaven and earth to answer our prayers which are often uttered, not in faith, but in a sort of superstitious hope.

God spends years in our lives trying to convince us of His goodness. We accept it to a certain extent but have a difficult time really embracing the concept. However, as we come into a fuller knowledge of God, our faith grows. As we see who He is, we trust Him more completely.

I have a good friend named Jerry who has four kids. He is a godly man with what seems to be an infinite amount of patience. When one of his kids misbehaves, he calmly and lovingly explains to them why they are about to be punished and then proceeds to dispense the required spanking. Typically, the kids see him as being a kind and loving father. If one of them needs something, they are not afraid to ask him. In fact, if it is something that they know to be a legitimate need, they ask with much confidence (perhaps too much sometimes!). Why do they have such confidence in him to grant their request? Jerry has proven his love and his kindness to them consistently over the years. They trust him because they know his character.

Isn't this exactly what Jesus teaches us in the Sermon on the Mount? He said, "Ask, and it shall be given to you; seek, and you shall find; knock, and it shall be opened to you. For everyone who asks receives, and he who seeks finds, and to him who knocks it shall be opened. Or what man is there among you, when his son shall ask him for a loaf, will give him a stone? Or if he shall ask for a fish, he will not give him a snake, will he? If you then, being evil, know how to give good gifts to your children, how much more shall your Father who is in heaven give what is good to those who ask Him!" (Matthew 7:7-11).

The basis for believing prayer isn't that we are able to grit our teeth and somehow conjure up sufficient faith to stifle all doubting thoughts. The foundation for believing God is our recognition of His goodness and His willingness to abundantly meet our needs.

The Greek word for believe is *pistos*. *Vine's Expository Dictionary* defines it as, "to believe, also to be persuaded of, and hence, to place confidence in, to trust, signifies, in this sense of the word, reliance upon, not mere credence."[6]

Another dictionary takes it even further when it considers the reason for the trust: "To persuade, particularly to move or affect by kind words or motives... To bring over to kind feelings, to conciliate... to pacify or quiet an accusing conscience... To win over, gain the favor of or make a friend of (someone)."[7]

These descriptions of the word believe remind me of the movie *Driving Miss Daisy*. In this movie, a Jewish woman in Georgia hires a black man as a chauffeur during the '50s. Deeply distrustful of all, cantankerous, and arrogant, the woman treats everybody around her with disdain. The black man, a devout Christian, continually humbles himself to her throughout their long relationship. At the end, as they have both grown old together, she lets her walls down for all to see her love and admiration for him. He won her heart by his humility and kindness.

This is a real picture of the way the Lord gets us to believe in Him. Year after year, He goes under us, helps us, encourages us, and blesses us. Eventually, the heart melts and He has won another to Himself. Only the hardest heart could resist such amazing love. For this reason, we must guard our hearts from straying away from Him.

Practical Application

Because I am cynical by nature I have had to incorporate several things into my life to keep myself in the light of His goodness.

First, I spend much time expressing gratitude and praise to the Lord.

Second, I constantly remind myself through the sermons and writings of godly ministers about the goodness and mercy of the Lord. I'm prone to forget how good God is and all that He has done for me.

Also, I try to frequently express my faith in the Lord. "I believe in you, Lord. I trust you. I know you are always helping me, sustaining me, keeping me. You are meeting my needs, taking me through and winning in my life. I trust you, Lord."

Words somehow create atmosphere. Have you ever been sitting in a room when someone walked in and began talking negatively about everything? Or what about when someone comes into a room in a rage, loudly cursing? In both instances an unpeaceful atmosphere is created.

It is also true in a positive way. Sometimes the men at the Pure Life residential program are encouraged to stand up in our meetings and praise the Lord for what He is doing in their lives. It increases their faith, and it also helps the others who are in the meeting as well. Words express "will," and "will" is spirit. When they stand up and say, "I will bless the Lord at all times," they are expressing their will to do so which affects the other men in a positive way at the same time.

Another thing that strengthens faith is the reading of the Word of God. Paul said, "So faith comes from hearing, and hearing by the word of Christ." (Romans 10:17)

And lastly, I must simply obey the Lord. Obedience deepens faith. As you read about the "Hall of Fame of Faith" found in Hebrews 11, you don't find any mention of signs and wonders. What you find as a common denominator of all of these heroes of the faith is a simple willingness to obey God.

All of these spiritual exercises deepen something in your heart so that when you call upon God, you have an assurance that He hears your prayers and is willing to respond.

The Place Of Repentance

More often than not, the deep trials and problems we face in life are because we have somehow gone our own way, outside of God's will. Addictive behavior, marital difficulties, and conflicts with other people usually revolve around not being controlled by the Holy Spirit.

As we begin to see more clearly what God is like in relation to what we're really like, a spiritual chemical reaction, if you will, begins to take place. Seeing God only makes us want to know Him better. Seeing ourselves only makes us want to be more like Him. Paul said that it is the kindness of God that leads people to repentance (Romans 2:4). Put it another way, God simply melts our hearts with His goodness. Knowing Him simply makes us want to do right!

Crying out to God for help before repentance occurs does absolutely no good. When we are in the wrong, we must first seek help by acknowledging our wrong and committing to go forward on the right path. Repentance is first turning away from our own way (sin and rebellion) and turning to the Lord.

Repentance gives us access into the kingdom of God. It comes first by seeing our need—or where we are wrong—and then by expressing heartfelt sorrow over that wrong. Only then are we restored into a right relationship with God.

The Pharaoh of Egypt prior to the Exodus provides a perfect example of what not to do. When Pharaoh refused to let the Hebrews leave, God brought pressure through plagues to relent. He pleaded for God's help, received it, and continued on in his sinful behavior. Does this remind you of anyone? We cry out to God to help us out of the terrible predicament we have gotten ourselves into. Out of sheer compassion He will often help us out. But the problem for some is that they never change the behavior that got them into a fix in the first place.

Take Jim, for instance. After years of emotionally abusing his wife and cheating on her with prostitutes, she finally left him. He cried out to God for help. He moaned, he sobbed, he wailed, he told anybody who would listen all his troubles. However, the one thing he would not do was repent of the behavior that caused the separation. Our counsel to her was that since he was showing no fruit of repentance she should stay separated from him until he did so. Tragically, to my knowledge, he never has.

God generally will not respond to the cries of a person in such an unrepentant state. It isn't that He does not feel for him and his plight, the Lord knows that until he will repent, nothing would be served by helping him. What best captures the attention of God are the words, "I am wrong." This is a person the Lord can help.

God's Response

A very phenomenal thing occurs in the heavenlies when one of God's children cries out for help in the right spirit. All heaven breaks loose in response! The closest thing I can think of in earthly terms would be a 911 response to a fire or to the scene of a car accident.

David, who had such wonderful revelations of God, experienced this firsthand when the Lord delivered him from sure death at the hands of Saul's henchmen. In a full heart of gratitude David wrote the Psalm 18. In this hymn of thanksgiving, he gives us a beautiful picture of God's response to the cry of the needy.

He begins by expressing what the Lord is to him:

> I love Thee, O LORD, my strength. The LORD
> is my rock and my fortress and my deliverer, my God,
> my rock, in whom I take refuge; my shield and the horn
> of my salvation, my stronghold. I call upon the LORD,
> who is worthy to be praised, and I am saved from my
> enemies.

He saw the Lord as his sufficiency. He then goes on to describe in vivid terms how he saw his situation in the spiritual realm:

> The cords of death encompassed me, and the torrents of ungodliness terrified me. The cords of Sheol surrounded me; the snares of death confronted me. In my distress I called upon the LORD, and cried to my God for help; He heard my voice out of His temple, and my cry for help before Him came into His ears.

What a wonderful testimony of God's faithfulness! The Lord was attentive to David's cries! In another Psalm he said, "The eyes of the LORD are toward the righteous, and His ears are open to their cry" (Psalms 34:5). This is something we desperately need to know in the dark days coming upon the earth.

> Then the earth shook and quaked; and the foundations of the mountains were trembling and were shaken, because He was angry. Smoke went up out of His nostrils, and fire from His mouth devoured; coals were kindled by it. He bowed the heavens also, and came down with thick darkness under His feet. And He rode upon a cherub and flew; and He sped upon the wings of the wind... The LORD also thundered in the heavens, and the Most High uttered His voice, hailstones and coals of fire. And He sent out His arrows, and scattered them, and lightning flashes in abundance, and routed them... He sent from on high, He took me; He drew me out of many waters. He delivered me from my strong enemy, and from those who hated me, for they were too mighty for me. They confronted me in the day of my calamity, but the LORD was my stay. He brought me forth also into a broad place; He rescued me, because He delighted in me.

No wonder toward the end he breaks into exuberant praise:

> The LORD lives, and blessed be my rock; and exalted be the God of my salvation... He delivers me from my enemies; surely Thou dost lift me above those who rise up against me; Thou dost rescue me

from the violent man. Therefore I will give thanks to Thee among the nations, O LORD, and I will sing praises to Thy name. He gives great deliverance to His king, and shows lovingkindness to His anointed, to David and his descendants forever.

I can relate to this Psalm. It is my testimony. "The snares of death confronted me. In my distress I called upon the LORD." He delivered me, gave me life, and destroyed my enemies! This is what He does for anyone who calls upon Him with a sincere heart.

The victorious believer must come to the place where he knows in his heart that victory comes only from the Lord. It is not something to be conjured up, nor does it occur simply because of some spoken claim to it. Spiritual victory comes about when a person learns to tap into the mighty powerhouse of God's mercy. This power is not available for the self-willed. It is only available for those who are willing to live in humble submission to God's will.

Meditation For Today

"The goodness of God breaking forth into a desire to communicate good was the cause and the beginning of the Creation. Hence, it follows that to all eternity God can have no thought or intent towards the creature but to communicate good, because He made the creature for this sole end, to receive good. The first motive towards the creature is unchangeable; it takes its rise from God's desire to communicate good, and it is an eternal impossibility that anything can ever come from God as His will and purpose towards the creature but the same love and goodness which first created it. He must always will that to which He willed at the creation of it. This is the amiable nature of God. He is the Good, the unchangeable, overflowing fountain of good that sends forth nothing but good to all eternity. He is the Love itself, the unmixed, immeasurable Love, doing nothing but from love, giving nothing but gifts of love to everything that He has made, requiring nothing of all His creatures but the spirit and fruits of that love which brought them into being. Oh, how sweet is this contemplation of the height and depth of the riches of Divine Love! With what attraction must it draw every thoughtful man to return love for love to this overflowing fountain of boundless goodness!"[1]

William Law

"You will never really know God's will until you get a real sight of Calvary—that was God's great exhibition of His will to this world."

Bill Vines

"For whoever does the will of My Father who is in heaven, he is My brother and sister and mother."[2]

Jesus Christ

"An unknown will of God is an unknown God... God's purpose for this earth was, and is, an immersion in a heavenly element, quite exactly the opposite of the spirit of the world which saturates the world with Force, and Wrath, and Corruption, Sin, Suffering, Pain, and Death... The will of God is mercy."[3]

Rex Andrews

Chapter Eleven

The Will of God

The quotes listed on the opposite page express such unspeakable riches that I feel there is little to add. If you would prayerfully meditate on these words, the truth expressed will become yours. God's intention for man is to do him good, not harm. His purpose for mankind is to give life, not death. His desire for people is only to help them, not hurt them. God's will toward mankind is always benevolent, good, and kind. His will is mercy.

Jesus Lived The Will Of God

In a previous chapter I said if you want to know what God is like, simply study the life of Jesus. If it is true that Jesus was God incarnate, then surely it is true that Jesus lived out the will of God. Jesus said, "My food is to do the will of Him who sent Me, and to accomplish His work" (John 4:34). He also said, "I can do nothing on My own initiative..." (John 5:30), and "... I always do the things that are pleasing to Him" (John 8:29). Everything Jesus did was an expression of God's will for mankind. God didn't show His good side in Jesus, while hiding a "bad" side.

God is not like us. The Lord is exactly what He expresses. However, we tend to present ourselves in a favorable light to look a certain way even if we're not really like that. How many of us live behind a facade of spirituality and contrived niceness, concealing the ugliness that most never see? The writer of Hebrews states that Jesus is "the exact representation of (God's) nature" (Hebrews 1:3). Jesus' life was an open book; He lived out the will of God toward man for all to see.

A late friend of mine said:

> Of Jesus it is written, "I come to do thy WILL, O God." (Hebrews 10:9) Jesus forgave sins by the will of God. He healed the sick by the will of God. He went to the cross to bear our sins and sickness BY THE WILL OF GOD. And so the Cross says, "God's will is mercy. God's will is benevolence. God's will is lovingkindness. God's will is redemption."[4]

In the ninth chapter of Matthew, we find the Master doing that very thing: living out mercy to those in need. After infuriating the mercy-opposing Pharisees by healing a paralytic and pardoning his sin. He comes upon a certain tax collector who later gave this firsthand account:

> And it happened that as He was reclining at the table in the house, behold many tax-gatherers and sinners came and were dining with Jesus and His disciples. And when the Pharisees saw this, they said to His disciples, "Why is your Teacher eating with the tax-gatherers and sinners?" When Jesus heard the Pharisees say this He responded, "It is not those who are healthy who need a physician, but those who are sick" (Matthew 9:11-12).

Now obviously what He is saying to these Pharisees is, "Only those who see their spiritual need want to hear from someone who can meet that need. You Pharisees see yourselves as good and don't see your need for help. That is why I came to be with the sinners."

Then Jesus says something that was downright revolutionary. "Go and learn what this means, I will have mercy, and not sacrifice:

for I am not come to call the righteous, but sinners to repentance"
(Matthew 9:13 KJV).

The Pharisees were in trouble. They were in spiritual delusion,
thinking they were in good standing before God. But Jesus told them
to do something: go study this verse from Hosea. They didn't realize
it but their eternity depended upon their willingness to humble
themselves and be taught. These men thought they knew. They saw
themselves as the experts. They already had everything figured out,
and their lives became a showcase for us on what not to do.

Jesus said, "Go and learn what this means..." It is imperative
to listen to and obey the commands of Jesus. We must be careful not
to think *we* know. What does this verse quoted from the book of
Hosea mean?

After several hundred years of corrupting the meaning of the
law given at Sinai, the Jews had turned the sacrificial system of burnt
offerings into a dead religion of external ceremonies. The original
purpose of the system was all mercy. It was a way for man to atone for
his sin, and draw close to God through heart-felt repentance and sacrifice.

After numerous painful centuries, the Lord sent a word to the
people, "For I desired mercy, and not sacrifice; and the knowledge
of God more than burnt offerings" (Hosea 10:12). What He was saying
was that if people really wanted to be in right fellowship with Him,
they needed to focus on the important issue: living out the love of
God to those around them. Jesus would later say to the Pharisees,
"Woe to you, scribes and Pharisees, hypocrites! For you tithe mint
and dill and cummin, and have neglected the weightier provisions of
the law: justice and mercy and faithfulness; but these are the things
you should have done without neglecting the others" (Matthew 23:23).

Something is weightier in God's scales than going through
the outward motions of religion (whether it be first-century Judaism
or 20th-century Christianity)—that His will is made known to man
and that people live it.

Jesus quoted the Scripture from Hosea from memory. He
said, "I will have mercy." To get the full and right sense of what was
said, the English supplied word "have" should be dropped: "I will
mercy." It is a statement of intent—what He wills to do for all
mankind. It is the will of God to do mercy and meet needs. It is also
His will that His followers do the same.

The Hosea passage states, "For I desired mercy, and not sacrifice; and the knowledge of God more than burnt offerings." Desire is will isn't it? If I say that it is my desire to drive to Cincinnati today, I am expressing my will, aren't I? Absolutely! Jesus is saying the same thing. It is the desire and will of God that mercy be done. This is the knowledge of God because it is the understanding of what He is like and of the Spirit He is in.

Whether you realized it or not when you picked up this book, you obeyed that very commandment. You are learning about the will of God in this book which is to do mercy, and His desire is that others do it too.

The devil is always trying to keep man from this knowledge. Whenever and wherever possible, he paints an almost irresistible picture that he's man's best friend while God is the real malefactor of this world. Then the devil win's man's friendship because he always appeals to his carnal, sinful, selfish nature. If I were a carnal Christian and the devil offered me a form of Christianity that would fit with that lifestyle, he would be my friend, whether I admitted it to others or not. If I were carnal and unwilling to repent, then I would discount the goodness of God, making Him into a big version of me—a "good" person.

We tend to give ourselves far too much credit. Again, we see ourselves as good people—not perfect like God perhaps—but doing fairly well. This same attitude that blinds us to our own need is what puts the knowledge of God out of our reach. As we actually see our desperate and needy condition, we also get a real sight of what God is truly like.

Satan duped Eve into believing that the knowledge of good and evil was the way to be like God—that God was holding out on her, holding out something valuable. In essence, Satan was saying, "The way to know God and be like Him is to have your eyes opened to all kinds of information." However, the Lord makes a faithful and true declaration: the entrance into the knowledge of God is through learning about mercy. One only comes into this knowledge through doing it—there are no shortcuts.

This knowledge will set you free of every bondage. Jesus said, "If you abide in My word, then you are truly disciples of Mine; and you shall know the truth, and the truth shall make you free" (John 8:31-32). What is the truth? That God is good, and His mercies are forever. If we live in this simple truth about God and live out this mercy to others, we shall be made free of every besetting sin.

The Subjection To A Higher Will

Meekness can be defined as the voluntary subjection of one person's will to that of another. Jesus said, "For I came down from heaven, not to do mine own will, but the will of him that sent me" (John 6:36 KJV). Jesus walked in perfect meekness—He walked in perfect subjection to the will of the Father. Even at His greatest crisis, where He took upon Himself the filthy sin of mankind, He said, "…nevertheless not my will, but thine, be done" (Luke 22:42 KJV).

Jesus lived in perfect surrender to the yoke of God. He trusted His Heavenly Father. Jesus knew God to be trustworthy. He believed in the Father. Jesus willingly subjected himself, knowing what it meant. Then He extended the offer to us to partake in the same yoke of subjection with Him. He said, "Come to Me, all who are weary and heavy-laden, and I will give you rest. Take My yoke upon you, and learn from Me, for I am gentle and humble in heart; and you shall find rest for your souls. For My yoke is easy, and My load is light" (Matthew 11:28-30).

We cringe when we think of someone putting a yoke upon us. In America, we are not accustomed to subjecting our wills to anybody. As a nation we pride ourselves on an independent spirit; we even celebrate the Fourth of July as the day we revolted against King George of England. Our independence, however, has grown to epic proportions in the last 30 years. The baby boomers of the '60s decided to throw off the yoke of authority in their lives. Thus began a cultural revolution that is still active today. People demand their freedom to the point that civil liberties are given far more weight in our court systems than the right to live in peace and safety. The outcome of this newfound freedom is the bondage of living in fear of crime, massive drug addiction, and a tidal wave of immorality.

What is freedom, and what is bondage? Many Christians try to have it both ways. They want the freedom of living their own lives, inviting God's presence on their terms, but never entering into the life of liberty in the Spirit that God intends for them. Undeniably lukewarm, they possess the worst of both worlds. They neither live in horrible, outward sin nor in the wedded bliss of the first love. Since they love their lives in this world, they will not abandon their lives to Jesus. Therefore, they do not really get to enjoy the pleasures of sin nor the glorious, overcoming life in the Spirit. Instead, they live in a dismal, gray world which exists between the two extremes—all under the nice sounding title of "being balanced." The reality is that they live in a spiritual ghetto.

Trusting His Will

When a person begins to understand God's will, the idea of living in obedience to Him is less terrifying. Hannah Whitall Smith lived a joy-filled life. In her book, *A Christian's Secret of a Happy Life*, she discusses the will of God:

> His will is the most blessed thing that can come to us under any circumstances. I do not understand how it is that the eyes of so many Christians have been blinded to this fact. But it really would seem as if God's own children were more afraid of His will than of anything else in life—His lovely, lovable will, which only means lovingkindnesses and tender mercies and blessings unspeakable to their souls! I wish I could show every one the immeasurable sweetness of the will of God. Heaven is a place of infinite bliss because His will is done there perfectly.[5]

A man may attempt to convince his friend that some activity is fun, safe, or enjoyable, but until that friend experiences it for himself, he will never know. Take a child who has never gone swimming. All his friends are doing it, and there is something appealing to him about it. But when he looks at the water, it terrifies him. The longer he stands there alongside the pool, the harder the others try to convince him. The more pressure he feels from them, the more he withdraws. Let his father get in that pool with his hands held out, and the little guy will then jump right into his daddy's arms. Why? Because he trusts his daddy. Time and again his father has shown his love for his son. I cannot convince you to throw yourself into the arms of God, but perhaps I can help you to see His trustworthiness. Oswald Chambers, who also knew something of the joy of the Lord in his life, said:

What is needed in spiritual matters is reckless abandonment to the Lord Jesus Christ, reckless and uncalculating abandonment, with no reserve anywhere about it; not sad, you cannot be sad if you are abandoned absolutely... Many of us are subtly serving our own ends, and Jesus Christ cannot help Himself to our lives; if I am abandoned to Jesus, I have no ends of my own to serve.[6]

Union Of Two Wills

In biblical times when two people were married, the woman understood that she was joining her life to her husband's. Today in America, marriage is more of an equal combining of two lives, two careers, two sets of desires. The role of the wife in biblical times was only a step above that of the family servant. The wife forfeited her dreams and aspirations to attach herself to the husband's. She became his mate and submitted her will to his. There was a union of two wills, but it was almost a complete subjection of one to the other.

We, as the Bride of Christ, are called to abandon our own interests, plans, and goals and subject them to our Lord and Husband. It is His responsibility to provide for us, protect us, and bring fulfillment to our lives. When we marry Him, we align our lives with His plans and submit our wills to His. It is part of the marriage agreement and to refuse to do it really does mean that, in some way, we have breached it.

Some men have a sincere desire to make this deeper consecration to the Lord, but feel as though they will not stick by it. One day they feel one way, the next another. It seems as though their emotions are continually being tossed around by the waves of life. What is needed is a prayer of consecration to the Lord, in spite of what we may feel later. Hannah Whitall Smith again:

Our will is the source of all our actions. Under the control of sin and self, our will caused us to act for our own pleasure. But God calls us to yield our wills to Him so He can take control of them and work in us to will and to do His good pleasure. If we will obey this call and present ourselves to Him as a living sacrifice, He will take possession of our surrendered wills, and will begin at once to work in us...

The will is like a wise mother in a nursery. The emotions are like crying children. The mother makes up her mind to have her children do what she believes to be right and best. The children complain and say they won't do it. However, the mother knows that she is the one in control and pursues her course lovingly and calmly in spite of all their complaints. The result is that the children are sooner or later won over to the mother's course of action. They fall in with her decision and all is harmonious and happy. But if for a moment that mother should think that the children were the masters instead of herself, confusion would reign. At this very moment there are many who are confused, simply because their feelings are allowed to govern instead of their will.[7]

God's Will In Our Lives

As I have already touched upon, one of our fears of consecrating ourselves to the will of God is that we don't trust His will. Rex Andrews addresses this:

People are prone to occupy their minds with many things about what God is going to do, and about His "power" meaning His destructive force, or power to overwhelm, so that His will seems to be that of an EARTHLY monarch, who depends upon force-to-kill in order to establish law. Human reasonings on Divine "power" are too apt to be SUPPOSITIONS of what His will really IS, unless it is kept clearly in view, all the time, what CALVARY means.[8]

As we gain knowledge of God's life-giving will, we will gradually begin to embrace it, indeed, abandon ourselves to it! What a wonderful thing it is, too. What is His will for you and I? Simply this: God is looking for men and women from all walks of life who will do His will to others as He has done to them. To put it into even stronger terms, He wills to possess people with His Holy Spirit and live out that life of the Spirit to others.

Just as self-righteousness is the biggest enemy of true righteousness, so self-will is the opposer and enemy to God's will. In self-will, we pick and choose when we would do mercy to others, to whom we will do mercy, and to what extent we will do it. God beckons us to lay it all down and simply allow Him to live out His life within us. We cannot be full of the Holy Spirit until we become emptied of self. We can have altar experiences where we are "filled with the Spirit." We can go to conferences about "walking in the Spirit." We can read books. We can delude ourselves into thinking we are being directed by the Holy Spirit, but until we come to the place of consecration where we abandon our wills and rights to God, we will never really know what it means to be full of the Spirit.

If you feel God's loving voice calling you right now, I encourage you to lay this book aside, go find a quiet spot and consecrate yourself to God. Make a full surrender of your life to Him, consciously subjecting yourself to His rightful authority over your life. You will never know victory until you do.

Perhaps the words of this Frances Havergal hymn will be of some assistance:

> Take my life, and let it be
> Consecrated, Lord, to Thee;
> Take my hands and let them move
> At the impulse of Thy Love.
> Take my feet, and let them be
> Swift and beautiful for Thee;
> Take my voice and let me sing
> Always, only, for my King.
> Take my silver and my gold,
> Not a mite would I withhold;
> Take my moments and my days,
> Let them flow in ceaseless praise.
> Take my will, and make it Thine,
> It shall be no longer mine;
> Take my heart, it is Thine own,
> It shall be Thy royal throne.[9]

Meditation For Today

"He that doeth the will of God abideth forever."[1]
The Apostle John

"Measure thy life by loss and not by gain, not by the wine drunk but by the wine poured forth; for love's strength standeth in love's sacrifice—and he who suffers most has most to give."[2]

Jonothan Goforth
(After losing five children
on the mission field)

"And let our people also learn to engage in good deeds to meet pressing needs, that they may not be unfruitful."[3]
The Apostle Paul

"Since there is a need, we must do what we can to meet it."
Betsy Ten Boom
in *The Hiding Place* (Movie)

Chapter Twelve

The Mercy Life

Having consecrated yourself to live out God's mercy, you are now faced with the question, "What does that mean in a practical way to my life?" You don't have to look far to find the answer. There are unmet needs everywhere you turn. Many inmates in jail would love to see Christian folks show an interest in them. Many retirees in rest homes would brighten up if someone would only care enough to visit them. Soup kitchens always need volunteers. Many drug rehabilitation facilities need men from the outside who are willing to help out. Most pastors have many positions to fill within their church: Sunday school workers, nursery workers, custodial services, parking lot attendants, or grounds keepers, to name a few. A person can be a blessing as a teacher's aide or a hospital volunteer. There is no shortage of opportunities for anyone desiring to invest his life, time and energy into the lives of others.

The whole life of Jesus was consumed with meeting others' needs. We call ourselves Christians, which makes us followers of Christ. And since He's the Leader, shouldn't we follow His lead?

The wonderful thing about the Christian life is that anybody can live it who's willing to. Anybody can be unselfish, from the smallest child to the oldest adult. True Christianity involves much more than simply learning information; it demands that every believer think and act according to the Word of God in his daily life.

Obligated To Do Mercy

Jesus gave a parable in Matthew 18 concerning forgiveness to explain and illustrate the kingdom of heaven. A slave owed a king a considerable amount of money. As was the custom in that day, when the debtor could not repay the money, he and his family were thrown into slavery until the debt could be paid. Distraught, the man threw himself at the feet of the king and begged for mercy. The king had compassion on him and forgave the debt.

This is a wonderful picture of our salvation. We have committed heinous crimes against a holy God. He brings us into His throne room and shows us what we have done. Guilty as charged, we see our need, our terrible predicament, and beg forgiveness.

Mercifully, God lifts the burden and releases us from our debt. But unfortunately, just like this slave, we begin to lose track of the great debt we were forgiven. Little by little, the pride that was dealt a blow when we first believed rears its ugly head again. No longer enraptured in that first love and in sight of our own need, we also gradually lose compassion for those around us. Before we know it, we have virtually no concern for the needs of others at all.

The slave saw a friend who owed him a few dollars. When the friend couldn't repay him, the slave had his friend thrown in prison. The king said to this slave, "Should you not also have had mercy on your fellow slave, even as I had mercy on you?" (Matthew 18:33).

Paul reminds us of our obligations: "... and He died for all, that they who live should no longer live for themselves, but for Him who died and rose again on their behalf... Therefore if any man is in Christ, he is a new creature; the old things passed away; behold, new things have come" (II Corinthians 5:15-17).

What is old? Selfishly living for one's own desires. What is new? Living for Christ and for others.

The apostle John also saw this. He said, "We know love by this, that He laid down His life for us; and we ought to lay down our lives for the brethren" (I John 3:16). Again, the same thing in other words: thinking about the needs of others.

Jesus said, "Heal the sick, raise the dead, cleanse the lepers, cast out demons; freely you received, freely give" (Matthew 10:8). What did they receive? Mercy! And so have we! Jesus came and met our needs, and He freely did it all. Freely you have had your needs met, now freely go and do the same.

This is the activity of the kingdom of God: doing for others and meeting their needs. These words are not given to us in some idealistic sermon that nobody is ever expected to really do. We are told expressly, "go and do the same." These are the practical words of Someone teaching us something very important: what it means to be His follower.

Counting The Cost

When Jesus first arrived on the scene in Palestine, a throng of ardent followers mobbed Him. They heard His gracious words of life, they saw His compassion and love, and they witnessed for themselves the power of God. Everyone wanted to be His follower although they were unaware of the price it would cost them. One day, Luke tells us, He looked over His shoulder and saw a "great multitude" following Him. He offered some words of advice for them:

> If anyone comes to Me, and does not hate his own father and mother and wife and children and brothers and sisters, yes, and even his own life, he cannot be My disciple. Whoever does not carry his own cross and come after Me cannot be My disciple. For which one of you, when he wants to build a tower, does not first sit down and calculate the cost, to see if he has enough to complete it? Otherwise, when he has laid a foundation, and is not able to finish, all who observe it begin to ridicule him (Luke 14:26-29).

These hard words separated the men from the boys, so to speak. These are the type of words no church growth pastor in his right mind would utter. Jesus wanted the people to know something. There was a cost involved with following Him. In America, we have managed to convince ourselves it's not true, but it is nonetheless.

The Sacrifice Of Mercy

Anyone determined to do a real work for God will be opposed

and persecuted. Those who tickle the ears of people will never have to deal with any real opposition.

There is a very good reason why John spoke of believers laying down their lives for each other, and why Paul spoke of being poured out as a drink offering. A person who loves others and does for others, makes himself vulnerable. When you care about people, you often get hurt. People turn on you, they lie about you, they use you, they steal from you, and they disappoint you. All of this is part and parcel for any real work of God. There are hardships sure to be faced to one degree or another for anybody living the mercy life.

There is usually little earthly reward for the true work of God, often times it is a sacrifice just doing it. Kathy and I both had to forfeit careers (law enforcement and management) for the sake of Pure Life Ministries. And when we did, we lost all. To obey the call of God we had to sell everything we owned and live in a motor home for several months. Later, when we first acquired the property where our ministry is now housed, we lived in a small camping trailer for a year and a half. I say this with some sense of shame when I think of the real sacrifice Christians in other nations face everyday. Recently the Lord provided the finances for us to build a nice, little house at the ministry, but it came after years of sacrifice. However, many mercy doers never receive such material blessings.

On top of all of this is the opposition one receives from the forces of hell. Demons bother very little with those who appeal to man's lower nature. When someone starts going the narrow way of living out the Christ-life for others, the devils of hell take notice. This is a very real part of any true work of God, but those doing this kind of work do not fear demons because they have seen God.

Suffering loss, sacrificing for others, feeling the stinging criticisms of detractors, being used by those you are trying to help, having things go wrong that shouldn't, and being hurt by those you are called to love are all part of living the mercy life. And yet, in some strange way, it is also part of the glory of the high calling. Christians are soldiers and their medals of valor are the scars they have suffered for their Savior.

The Benefits Of Living Mercy

In the unseen realm of the kingdom of heaven, there are very tangible rewards for those who will love other people. Many will never know the rich blessings of this life because, in their spiritual dimness, all they can see are the requirements and losses involved. Nevertheless, the benefits of spiritual victory that come from doing mercy to others are beyond our ability to fully comprehend.

A friend of mine once said the following:

> The Lord seems close when we are conscious of the need around us. If He seems far away it's because the need of others has become unimportant to you. The need puts you in touch with Jesus. This is how to be like Jesus. When you feel like He is distant, it's because the needs of others are dead in your heart. There is no way your heart can be dead to the Lord when you are reaching out to others.

I have certainly found this to be true. One of the benefits of helping others is that the Lord draws very close. Why is that? For one thing, when you are meeting needs, you are like a glove filled with the hand in operation. Jesus fills you and does what He loves to do through you. You are taking an interest in His most prized possession: people. Nobody gets the attention of the Lord like those in need.

The person filled and used by the Spirit to meet other's needs walks in a depth of spiritual authority. We will discuss this in more detail in a later chapter.

We come into the knowledge of God by doing good to others. It is what God is in and what He is doing. This, more than anything, draws us close to Him. As John said, "The one who does not love does not know God, for God is love" (I John 4:8). It is simply a fact that we do not know God any more than we are living out His love to others.

There is also a spiritual law that comes into effect as a person lives in mercy toward others. Paul said, "...for whatever a man sows, this he will also reap" (Galatians 6:7). Jesus said it this way, "...by your standard of measure, it will be measured to you" (Matthew 7:2).

These words are meant for us in this life. If you are giving nothing out in life, according to this spiritual law, you are receiving nothing. If you are giving out very little, you can expect to receive little. However, if you are giving out all you have, you have placed yourself in the position to receive abundance in return. As Jesus said, "Be merciful, just as your Father is merciful.... Give, and it will be given to you; good measure, pressed down, shaken together, running over, they will pour into your lap. For by your standard of measure it will be measured to you in return" (Luke 6:36-38).

These words were not given in the context of material gain from some God-manipulating scheme. The whole context of this passage is loving others and doing mercy. When you live your life to bless the lives of others, you are going to be blessed. It is that simple. The ways you will be blessed are innumerable. The Psalmist revealed this when he said, "How blessed is he who considers the helpless; the LORD will deliver him in a day of trouble. The LORD will protect him, and keep him alive, and he shall be called blessed upon the earth... The LORD will sustain him upon his sickbed; in his illness, Thou dost restore him to health" (Psalm 41:1-3). How do you put a price tag on that kind of divine blessing?

Our judgment is contingent upon what we do for others. Jesus used the illustration of the sheep and the goats to show this truth. Those illustrated as sheep fed the hungry, gave drink to the thirsty, showed hospitality to the stranger, clothed the naked, helped the sick, and visited the prisoner. Those labeled as goats had no time for such things. We know from Scripture that good works do not earn us a place in heaven, and yet, it seems very clear that good works are the fruit revealing that a person has truly been converted. For instance, consider what Jesus said:

> Enter by the narrow gate; for the gate is wide, and the way is broad that leads to destruction, and many are those who enter by it. For the gate is small, and the way is narrow that leads to life, and few are those who find it.
>
> Beware of the false prophets, who come to you in sheep's clothing, but inwardly are ravenous wolves. You will know them by their fruits. Grapes are not gathered from thorn bushes, nor figs from thistles, are they? Even so, every good tree bears good fruit; but the bad tree bears bad fruit. A good tree cannot produce

bad fruit, nor can a bad tree produce good fruit. Every
tree that does not bear good fruit is cut down and
thrown into the fire. So then, you will know them by
their fruits.

Not everyone who says to Me, "Lord, Lord,"
will enter the kingdom of heaven; but he who does the
will of My Father who is in heaven. Many will say to
Me on that day, "Lord, Lord, did we not prophesy in
Your name, and in Your name cast out demons, and in
Your name perform many miracles?" And then I will
declare to them, "I never knew you; depart from Me,
you who practice lawlessness" (Matthew 7:13-23).

James later backed this up when he wrote about saving faith:

For judgment will be merciless to one who has
shown no mercy; mercy triumphs over judgment. What
use is it, my brethren, if a man says he has faith, but he
has no works? Can that faith save him? If a brother or
sister is without clothing and in need of daily food,
and one of you says to them, "Go in peace, be warmed
and be filled," and yet you do not give them what is
necessary for their body, what use is that? Even so
faith, if it has no works, is dead, being by itself... You
believe that God is one. You do well; the demons also
believe, and shudder (James 2:13-19).

Real believers don't get involved in the needs of others
because they fear going to hell. Because they believe, they give
themselves over to serving and helping people. They neither consider
the benefits of doing mercy nor the consequences of refusing to do
mercy. They are simply compelled by God's love inside them.

False Mercy

We have talked a lot in this book about mercy and what it
means from a biblical perspective. We must now also put to rest
incorrect notions about mercy.

Anything done in the name of mercy that puts temporal needs

before eternal is not of God. When Jesus was hanging on the cross, a number of people were coaxing Him to come down. Where would we be today had they succeeded? This happens today as well. Sometimes God deals with His children very strongly. Then some well-meaning soul comes along and sees a brother going through the discipline of the Lord and tries to coax him off the cross Jesus has just given him to bear.

A man in our residential program was very much full of this kind of false mercy. In this program God corrects the men for their own good. Men would never change were it not for that correcting process. In fact, the process of correction is God's mercy to them, but this man could hardly take it when he saw others being dealt with strongly by God. He wanted everybody to have the same shallow happiness he had. He simply had no comprehension of the way God helps people through adversity. So, in his own emotional, fleshly way, he was forever trying to patch up wounds that God had inflicted! He had to be taught that sometimes mercy seems cruel, but it is exactly what the person needs at that time and therefore is mercy for them.

Another example of false mercy is pity on one person at the expense of others. There was a time in this country when a convicted murderer was taken out and hanged within a few days of his conviction. Occasionally an innocent man was executed. In the name of mercy activists took up the cause to stop this from ever happening again and have lengthened the process from a few days to around ten years. Now these activists are trying to do away with capital punishment completely under the pretense that it is not a deterrent to crime. Of course it's not a deterrent to crime! They have made it so hard to convict a murderer, have him sentenced to death, and have that execution actually take place that common criminals have practically no fear of the law anymore.

Yes, it is true that since the liberals have had their way in our court system, fewer innocent people have been convicted of crimes. But the trade-off for this small handful (that are usually criminals in the wrong place at the wrong time) that have benefited are millions being victimized every day across the country because crime is running so rampant. The liberals have had their way to the point that the criminal's rights far exceed those of the average innocent citizen. This is not mercy.

Mercy for all would be to have a judicial system that puts fear into those thinking about committing a crime. This may seem hard-nosed, but it really is the merciful thing for everybody involved.

Another example of false mercy is seen when a person appeases sinful manipulation. Is it merciful to give a kid a toy because he throws a tantrum? Would it be merciful for a girl to marry a man she does not love because he threatens to commit suicide if she doesn't? Would it be merciful for a counselor at Pure Life Ministries to let a student have his own way when he knows it will harm him? Of course, the answer to all of these questions is no. Mercy meets needs, not the sinful manipulation of someone who simply wants his own way.

The following song by Ira B. Wilson would make a wonderful prayer:

Make Me a Blessing
Out in the highways and byways of life,
Many are weary and sad;
Carry the sunshine where darkness is rife,
Making the sorrowing glad.

Tell the sweet story of Christ and His love,
Tell of His pow'r to forgive;
Others will trust Him if only you prove
True, every moment you live.

Give as 'twas given to you in your need,
Love as the Master loved you;
Be to the helpless a helper indeed,
Unto your mission be true.

Chorus
Make me a blessing,
Make me a blessing,
Out of my life...
May Jesus shine;
Make me a blessing,
O Savior, I pray,
Make me a blessing to someone today.[4]

Meditation For Today

"If we love God and give ourselves to Him, we must give ourselves to the whole world. Otherwise we would divide off our personal experience of God from His Greatness and Infinite Presence and turn what ought to be dedication into private enjoyment.

"One of the holy miracles of love is that once it is really started on its path, it cannot stop; it spreads and spreads in ever-widening circles till it embraces the whole world in God. We begin by loving those nearest to us, end by loving those who seem farthest. And as our love expands, so our whole personality will grow, slowly but truly. Every fresh soul we touch in love is going to teach us something fresh about God.

"One of the mystics said: God cannot lodge in a narrow heart: our hearts are as great as our love. Let us take that into our meditation and measure our prayer and service against the unmeasured generosity of God."[1]

Evelyn Underhill

"If you are devoted to the cause of humanity, you will soon be exhausted and have your heart broken by ingratitude, but if the mainspring of your service is love for Jesus, you can serve men although they treat you as a door-mat."[2]

Oswald Chambers

Where'er you ripened fields behold
Waving to God their sheaves of gold,
Be sure some corn of wheat has died,
Some saintly soul been crucified:
Someone has suffered, wept, and prayed,
And fought hell's legions undismayed.[3]

A.S. Booth Clibborn

"Blessed are the merciful, for they shall receive mercy."[4]

Jesus Christ

Chapter Thirteen

Doers Of Mercy

In a chapter about the lives of people who have lived out God's mercy, you might expect stories of great men and women of God who have lived down through the centuries. Certainly there are many examples of those whom God raised up to meet a need. To exotic India, steeped in the heathen practices of Hinduism, God sent William Carey who spent 41 years there, translating the entire Bible into six languages, and portions into 29 other tongues. For dark, foreboding Africa, with its disease-infested water, dangerous wildlife, and uncharted jungles, God raised up David Livingstone who spent his entire life exploring the continent and evangelizing the people.

In the last century, God sent Mother Teresa to the slums of Calcutta, Jackie Pullinger to the drug addicts of Hong Kong, Brother Andrew to the forgotten believers behind the Iron Curtain, and David Wilkerson to the gangs of New York City. These and more have been raised up by God to touch the lives of needy people. Their lives embody the victorious Christian life to its fullest.

Instead of retelling their well-know stories, I felt the Lord leading me to share the stories of certain mercy doers that I know personally. I understand the wisdom in this. First, I know their stories intimately. I don't have to rely on the observations of others.

Second, and perhaps much more importantly, they are not "great men and women but average individuals like you and me whom God has touched. They are people we can relate to. You probably would never relate to someone like Martin Luther, but you can relate to these stories. Having said all that, let's look at the lives of these four men and their wives who have been willing to be used by the Lord.

The ministry of Nelson Hinman spanned 62 years. I was among a privileged few asked to speak at his retirement dinner in 1995. Little did I know then that he would go on to be with his beloved Savior within a year.

After serving a stint in the navy, Nels began to preach under the name of "The Sailor Evangelist." Before long, he was in demand all around the country. In 1944 he was asked to become the pastor of the prestigious Bethel Temple, in Sacramento, one of the largest churches in California. While serving there he became chaplain to the California Senate.

Nels had a charismatic personality, but his wife knew what he was like behind closed doors. The person she knew was often much different than the lovable pastor everybody else saw. Pastor Hinman had a real anger problem. "There were times I would be in a rage against my wife and someone would come to the door and I would instantly be transformed into the most gracious person alive. You could have never guessed that a moment before I was going on one of my tirades against my wife."

After 29 years of marriage, Mrs. Hinman had seen enough of hypocrisy; seething bitterness had slowly built up in her heart. One day he came home and she had simply vanished. It would be some time before Nels found out she had run off with another man. Nobody was more shocked than Nels. He had been in such a state of delusion about his behavior, he didn't even know there was a problem in their marriage.

Some years later, well into his second marriage, he discovered that this wife, too, was about to leave him. He was mystified. It was then one of his close friends asked him, "Did you ever stop to think that the problem might be you?"

Nels Hinman became determined to get the personal help he needed. This course eventually brought him into contact with a man named John Broger, an ex-navy intelligence officer who taught people how to overcome their problems through biblical principles. The subject fascinated Nels. The more he studied, the more hope began to rise within his heart that not only could he overcome his anger problem, but that people could overcome any problem using the principles found in Scripture.

Eventually his second wife died. It was about this time he wrote *An Answer To Humanistic Psychology* which was published by Harvest House. Over the next few years, Nels began teaching biblical counseling techniques in different churches throughout California. While in Redding, he became interested in one of his students who herself had just been recently widowed. Nels and Juanita tied the knot in 1985.

Nels was a different husband this time around. Anybody who spent time around these two knew very well how sweetly he treated her. For instance, he determined that his wife should never have to open a door for herself if he were around. These small kindnesses revealed the change which occurred in his heart. Not once did Juanita experience the anger the first two wives came to know so well. If he hadn't been so open about the way anger had ruled his earlier life, she would have never guessed.

Later that year the newlyweds came to Sacramento and were invited on a daily radio show on KFIA. The general manager of the station was so impressed with what they were teaching that he offered them a daily hour slot on his station. *Heart Talk* radio show was founded.

These were happy years for Nels and Juanita. During the day, when they weren't teaching in a local Bible school (where an eager student named Steve Gallagher was attending) and hosting the daily talk show, the Hinmans put in long hours of counseling.

When Nels married Juanita, she had a savings account that had provided her with a sense of security for her retirement. Since they never charged for their counseling and donations didn't cover the enormous radio program bills, they quickly went through her entire savings. For years they lived on very little so they could be a help to others.

The radio show was immensely popular in Sacramento. This was made evident by the long list of people who wanted to come to them for counseling. One day, the secretary said, "Are you aware that we are booking appointments three months in advance?"

Nels could hardly take this. "That's like going to the hospital with a ruptured appendix and being told to come back in three months!"

The Hinmans decided to begin teaching marriage classes, and make attendance mandatory for any couple who wanted counseling. The teaching was so good that marital problems were dissolving during the six weeks of classes.[5]

Finding adequate space for the classes became a problem. People frustrated with the lack of results through conventional "Christian" psychology were fascinated with the biblical concepts they heard. Soon, folks from all over northern California were attending. Nels and Juanita also began teaching lay people how to counsel other believers using the Word of God. Training others to counsel relieved the Hinmans of the tremendous burden of those needing biblical counseling.

For some 10 years, despite tremendous opposition in the Christian community, Nels Hinman stood firm in his belief that the Bible should be the only source for answers to people's problems. I Corinthians 4:6, "Never beyond what is written," became the show's motto. His radio program, which featured on-the-air counseling, taught people every day that God could be trusted to handle their difficulties. We cannot know the full impact of *Heart Talk* on the Sacramento Christian community. Many people were taught how to live in victory by applying scriptural principles and standards to their daily lives.

God used the life of Nels Hinman in a tremendous way to meet the needs of those around him—his was a life of mercy. Many grateful attendees both at his retirement dinner and at his funeral were real life testimonies of lives changed and affected by his love for the truth.

At first glance the story of Dick Engel might seem out of place in this chapter. He has never been in full-time ministry and indeed, doesn't see himself in that light. Raised in a United Church of Christ, Dick always assumed that he was leading a Christian life. When he married, he and his wife Kathy began attending a United Church of

Christ. It was all he had ever known.

"It was not long after we began attending that church that Kathy began having strange experiences with God," he says. I didn't understand what was going on; neither did our pastor." Under heavy conviction by the Holy Spirit, Kathy found the Lord, but it would be nearly a year before Dick would see his need.

Once they were saved, they immersed themselves in the needs of the church. "God gave us a real love for the kids. We taught Sunday school and got involved with the youth fellowships. It wasn't long before we were totally caught up in the lives of the young people."

With a real heart for ministry, Kathy hoped they might one day co-pastor a church, but Dick never felt comfortable with the idea. "I always wanted to be in the ministry of helps. The pastor can't do everything himself. He needs people who are willing to help him. I would rather be in the background doing what I can to help out."

Dick and Kathy eventually ended up in Cincinnati, Ohio. Kathy worked as a registered nurse, Dick as a manager of a picture frame factory in Florence, Kentucky. It was in this capacity that we at Pure Life became acquainted with Dick.

The men in Pure Life's live-in program hold down outside employment during their six-month stay. Most of them obtain work through local temporary agencies with whom we have established relationships. An employer calls them asking for workers, and the temporary agency is paid a fee for each acceptable worker they provide.

Over the years we have worked with a number of employers, but never any quite like Dick Engel. "When I would call Dick and tell him about a guy we needed to place, I would be totally honest with him about the problems we had had with him," one of our counselors related to me. "Most of the guys we have sent him are the ones that nobody else would hire. He has never turned away any of our guys."

Most of the men in the live-in program come from typical, working backgrounds. They have held jobs all their lives and being employed through a temporary agency is not a problem. Occasionally, however, we get a difficult case in here; those who for a variety of reasons cannot seem to hold down a job. One guy has a hard time getting along with other people. Another one cannot work hard due to some physical limitation. Someone else has a hard time comprehending simple orders. Every time we have had someone difficult to place, Dick Engel has been willing to hire him.

It doesn't end there, though. Not only has he been willing to hire these tough cases, he has involved himself in their lives. "One thing I appreciate about Dick is that the interests of the guys always comes before the business," our counselor shared with me. "If he had to make a decision about one of the guys, he would always call us first to make sure it wouldn't have some detrimental effect on his life."

His patience with difficult people is almost legendary at Pure Life. Some of those we have sent him cannot seem to get along with anybody. Dick welcomes them with the open arms of a loving father. He works with them, willing to be longsuffering with even the most troublesome employees. It isn't that he is just willing to accept and tolerate the hard cases; he calls us up and asks for them!

There are times when our guys have personality clashes on the job. Dick remains unruffled. He simply gets the men together and talks it out with them. He has a real ability to bring peace into even the most stressful situations. He provides a calming presence in the workplace. The guys trust him.

Dick Engel is a very unique man. What makes him special is simply his willingness to love people as the Lord has loved him.

Robert Carrillo experienced one of the most radical transformations I have seen in all my years of ministry. Married with four children, Robert was a hopeless drug addict in Sacramento. His addiction had made him so extremely selfish that he would steal welfare money and food stamps from his wife to buy drugs, leaving her to rummage through garbage cans to feed the kids.

One day, while driving his motorcycle down the street, Robert was pulled over for speeding. When the officer radioed to the dispatcher, word came back that Robert had seven warrants for his arrest. The policeman knew he had a bad character on his hands. As he was preparing to arrest Robert, the Lord spoke to the Christian officer not to arrest him but to tell him about Jesus. Before the encounter was over, Robert had given his life to Christ.

The officer later directed Robert to the largest church in the area, Trinity Church in Sacramento. Coincidentally a guest evangelist was speaking about ministering to the homeless. Robert understood homelessness because he had been without shelter many times in his life. Those who attended the conference spent Saturday feeding vagrants congregated down at skid row. After the conference ended, the evangelist left town to go on to his next destination.

For Robert, however, it was only the beginning. The next morning he went back down to skid row and picked up 22 men and brought them into the luxurious sanctuary of Trinity Church. The folks at the church that day were shocked. These guys were raw—smelly and scraggly in appearance.

As evening came around, the time came for Robert to take the men back down to skid row, but he just couldn't do it. He looked at Beverly, his wife, to tell her about the problem, but God had already spoken to her. "I know, Robert. The Lord already told me. You're bringing them home."

That evening Robert brought all 22 men into his two-bedroom apartment. The kids slept in their parent's room, and the men slept anywhere they could find a spot. The Lord's House ministry to the homeless opened that night.

Over the next several years, Pastor Leroy Lebeck of Trinity had much to deal with. "When these guys first began to follow the Lord, sometimes the old nature would come out and there were fights—sometimes knife fights in the church parking lot. I began wondering what we had gotten ourselves into and whether we needed bouncers at church instead of ushers."

Robert himself was in thirteen fights at the church during the first couple of years of ministry. Through it all, Pastor Lebeck stood by Robert, even when some were calling for the pastor to kick him out of the church. After what would turn out to be his last fight, Robert went to Pastor Lebeck and confessed that he had done it again.

"Robert, did you kill him?"

"No, it wasn't too bad this time."

"Well, things are getting better."

Early on, Robert and Bev began going to the counseling classes led by Nels and Juanita Hinman. Gradually, through the patience of the staff at Trinity, the personal help of the Hinmans, and the work of the Holy Spirit, Robert and Bev began changing.

Today, the Carrillo's ministry provides 15,000 meals each month. They give out over 8,000 of those meals to the transients on skid row. Hundreds of food boxes are made up for working families "so they can afford to purchase clothes for their kids and other things they normally wouldn't be able to afford." On top of all of that, they run a discipleship program in a renovated downtown mansion.

"Our goal," says Bev, "is to share with others like we were shared with in the past and to teach them the value of the love of Christ."

Surely the lives of Robert and Beverly Carrillo are shining examples of God living out His mercy to the needy of this world.

Jimmy Jack grew up in a large, troubled family in Long Island, New York. By the time he entered high school, he was abusing hard drugs and had five felony convictions. For the next several years, Jimmy tried to fill the insatiable hunger of his addiction. One night, it almost ended in tragedy.

"My best friend Billy and I went to the Lower East Side of Manhattan and bought four bags of heroin. I snorted one bag; then held Billy's arm as he injected three bags. Billy overdosed and life began to leave him. I tried everything I could to help save him but to no avail. The only thing left was to call out to God. So I cried out to God and miraculously paramedics came out of nowhere. They began doing CPR on him, trying to save him. I heard them say, 'he's gone.' I begged them to keep working as I got on my knees on the side of that van and cried aloud, 'Oh God, save Billy and I will commit my entire life to you.' Suddenly Billy came alive!"

Even though he promised his life to God, Jimmy continued on the same path. Totally ashamed over his broken commitment, he tried to quiet his conscience with more drugs. Things got even worse. One day, someone stole the van he lived in. It contained everything he owned. Jimmy, feeling like he couldn't take anymore, went out and got high on crack cocaine, eventually ending up in a bar in some run down neighborhood. It wasn't long before the effects of the alcohol kicked in as well. His depression turned into anger.

At the other end of the bar sat another guy down on his luck. He, too, had an attitude, and the two locked into hateful stares. Jimmy was carrying a sharpened screwdriver and started toward the guy to stab him. Suddenly an old friend named George walked in and saw what was happening. He ran over to Jimmy and threw his arms around him, warning him not to "do something stupid." Jimmy broke and George took him to a Teen Challenge Center, a Christian facility for drug addicts.

After three months in the program Jimmy married his girlfriend Miriam and eventually they went on to an Assembly of God Bible college. Upon graduation in 1989, Jimmy returned to New York and founded Long Island Teen Challenge. Since that time, the ministry has expanded to include a church of 500, a men's home which houses 30, and a woman's home which houses 15.

But the real story of Jimmy Jack isn't found in the size of the ministry, but in the size of his heart.

"Jimmy Jack never gives up on a person," says Jeff Colon, director of the Pure Life live-in program. "He was always willing to work with me." Jeff should know, having gone through his program before coming to Pure Life. "He's constantly involved with other people's problems. He's got such a heart for people he's willing to do whatever it takes to help them. It doesn't matter what it costs him."

This meant a lot to Jeff's wife Rose, who often called Jimmy and Miriam in the middle of the night, because of Jeff's problems with drug addiction. "It didn't matter what time of day or night. I knew when I called that they wouldn't consider me a bother," recalls Rose. "They were there for me."

Another illustration of Jimmy's heart for people is seen in the street crusades he holds in ghetto areas every summer. "Sometimes the atmosphere would be charged with hostility," recalls Jeff. "There were times people would even throw bottles at Jimmy while he was preaching, but Jimmy's the sort of guy who is oblivious to people's hatred. He just keeps telling them they need Jesus."

The lives of Jimmy and Miriam Jack are further examples of God living out His great love through vessels of mercy toward those deemed unlovable by everyone else.

Indeed, these precious saints are examples of the life of victory available to the believer. Christianity is manifested by its outward works, but there is another aspect of the mercy life that no one else but God sees.

Meditation For Today

"If you can beat the devil in the matter of regular, daily prayer, you can beat him anywhere. If he can beat you there, he can beat you anywhere."

Anonymous

"Prayer is taxing. Prayer is exacting. Prayer means enduring. Prayer means denying self, a daily dying by choice... (But) Shall we render unto the Lord that which costs us nothing? We will have to sacrifice precious things in our lives if we are going to learn the great art of intercession."[1]

Leonard Ravenhill

"It has often been said that prayer is the greatest force in the universe. This is no exaggeration. It will bear constant repetition. In this atomic age when forces are being released that stagger the thought and imagination of man, it is well to remember that prayer transcends all other forces."[2]

F.J. Huegel

"Since only the white light of Calvary's power can dissipate the black workings of hell, the only people who can change bleak circumstances and reverse the tide of encroaching evil wherever it rises are those who pray in Jesus' name.

"But sloth is the earmark of Adam's race when it comes to spiritual responsibility. We would rather blame God than trust Him; rather complain about Him than call upon Him. How many would rather indict the Almighty for neglect when hell comes against us, than invite His almightiness to eject the hell-worker?"[3]

Jack Hayford

Chapter Fourteen

The Prayer Of Mercy

Kathy and I are about as different in our personalities as two people can be. She is light-hearted and fun-loving while I tend to be serious and industrious. She is a "people-person." I am happy to be holed up in a room somewhere with a computer. She is stable and balanced. I am driven, forceful, and sometimes reckless.

However, there is no place that the differences in our personalities tend to stand out more than in our prayer lives. I am a "prayer-walker." In the last 15 years, I have walked close to 12,000 miles in prayer. That's a lot of shoe rubber! I have walked between the pews in churches, up and down dark streets in the wee hours of the morning, through parks, along golf courses, in the woods, through pastures and around malls. Wherever I am in the country, I get up in the morning, have my coffee as I study the Bible and then go out for my usual prayer walk. It is the easiest way for me to connect with God.

Kathy's prayer life has developed in a different way. Every day, she sits in bed and writes her prayers down in a small binder. Over the course of years the pages have accumulated to the point of filling up a whole box. She cannot seem to throw them away!

When I saw that box of prayers, it occurred to me how precious they are to God. In Revelation, we are told that when the seventh seal is broken, the prayers of the saints will be poured out upon the golden altar before the throne and, along with burning incense, will go up before God. In the Bible, aroma and fragrance are always symbolic of sacrifice. This is what is so precious in the eyes of the Lord.

The prayer that avails much in heaven is sacrificial in nature. *If mercy is the meeting of another's needs, then mercy-praying is the appeal to God to meet the needs for the person which we do not have the resources to meet ourselves.* We go to God on behalf of another, asking Him to meet that person's needs as He sees fit.

Praying With Authority

The secret of answered prayer is to pray according to the will of God. Jesus said,

> Truly, truly, I say to you, he who believes in Me, the works that I do shall he do also; and greater works than these shall he do; because I go to the Father. And whatever you ask in My name, that will I do, that the Father may be glorified in the Son. If you ask Me anything in My name, I will do it. If you love Me, you will keep My commandments (John 14:12-15).

When Jesus said that He would do whatever is asked in His name, does that mean I can ask for a Cadillac to be delivered to my front door? We have all found out through unanswered prayers that there is something more to the principle of praying in His name than just ending our prayers with, "...in the name of Jesus."

What *does* it mean to pray in the name of Jesus?

It seems that Pure Life Ministries is always involved in building projects. In our first five years alone—generally with a crew of three or four workers at a time—we constructed seven buildings, two barns, and set up two trailers. I can say it was all done with a pocketful of change, little help, and a mustard seed of faith.

There have been many times that one of our guys needed to go into town to purchase some materials. Typically, when that happens, I send him off with a signed check made out to the store to get what he needs. All he has to do is fill in the amount. Often I don't even know what he is going after.

This is a good illustration of petitioning God in the name of Jesus. We have been given a blank check with the signature of Jesus Christ scrawled on the bottom. This check authorizes us to buy whatever we need for the project we are working on. This check is accepted, not because of our trustworthiness, but because the signature on the bottom of the check is respected. If I send one of our workers to the store to pick up some paint, they approve the check, not because they know the worker, but because they know Pure Life Ministries will make good on that check.

In the same way, it is by Jesus' name that our petitions are stamped "APPROVED" when they are presented in heaven; because of the respect of the name appearing upon that request rather than because of our merit.

What do you suppose would happen if one of our workers showed up at Wal-Mart and, instead of buying the paint, went on a wild spending spree buying himself clothes, sports equipment, dress shoes, a television and video recorder? Do you think the Wal-Mart employee might be suspicious?

The name of Jesus simply means that we are going to the store in heaven to purchase what He has sent us to purchase. We are praying in His will. John said, "And this is the confidence which we have before Him, that, if we ask anything according to His will, He hears us. And if we know that He hears us in whatever we ask, we know that we have the requests which we have asked from Him" (I John 5:14-15). What is His will? That the needs of others are met. You can never go wrong praying for the needs of others! However, the same cannot be said about self-centered prayers. James said, "You ask and do not receive, because you ask with wrong motives, so that you may spend it on your pleasures" (James 4:3).

Crisis Intervention

Intercession means we go to God, intervening on the behalf of others. The real picture of this is that of a defense attorney who goes to the judge representing his client. Take this even a step further: an attorney who represents poor people at his own expense because they cannot afford to pay him. He sees the need and accepts the responsibility of that person's need upon himself. Once he agrees to take the case, he has committed himself to see it through. He will do everything within his power to adequately represent his client. He bears the person's need upon himself.

Suppose an elderly couple was robbed of their life's savings by a fast-talking con-artist who has grown rich by swindling the unsuspecting. The attorney feels compassion for them and agrees to take the case free-of-charge. He does all of the legwork on the case, finds the con man, and locates the bank accounts where he has stashed his money. The attorney puts his heart into it. His compassion for the elderly couple compels him to treat this case as if he were being paid top dollar for taking it on. His actions, of course, are mercy—meeting the need of someone else.

There is one other crucial player in this story: the judge. In this scenario, the judge is a benevolent, elderly man who also feels compassion for the couple. He understands their plight. He is committed to seeing justice done in their case. So, just to make sure the attorney doesn't short-change the couple by asking for too little compensation, he secretly and subtly lets the lawyer know that he is very receptive to their case. Of course, it would be unethical to come right out and say it, but he makes sure the lawyer figures it out.

When the lawyer is finally able to go before the judge to seek damages, do you think he will be satisfied to receive the bare minimum for these people? No! He will be pleading their cause before the judge, requesting sizeable compensation. Prior knowledge of the kind intentions of the judge drives him on and gives him the confidence he needs in court.

When we take another man's problems upon ourselves in prayer, in essence we become his legal counsel. We pray because we see his need and feel compassion for him because of it. Such compassion drives us to seek God on his behalf over and over if necessary. We leave no stone unturned in our diligence to see that need met. When we go before God, we do not seek a small answer— we seek a large answer! The Lord tells us that He looks very favorably upon any requests that come His way on behalf of those in need. We do not go before God looking for a tablespoon worth of living waters, we plead for a deluge!

Anatomy Of Intercessory Prayer

One day the disciples asked Jesus to teach them how to pray.

After sharing with them the Lord's prayer (which is all mercy), He told them a story.

> Suppose one of you shall have a friend, and shall go to him at midnight, and say to him, "Friend, lend me three loaves; for a friend of mine has come to me from a journey, and I have nothing to set before him;" and from inside he shall answer and say, "Do not bother me; the door has already been shut and my children and I are in bed; I cannot get up and give you anything." I tell you, even though he will not get up and give him anything because he is his friend, yet because of his persistence he will get up and give him as much as he needs (Luke 11:5-8).

What a wonderful picture of how prayers get answered in the kingdom of God. There are six different points to draw out of this story.

First, the person who comes to him is a friend. We are not called to save the whole world. We are asked to take the burdens of those who come into our lives with needs. Whether the person is actually a friend or just someone we know about does not matter. When we take their need upon ourselves, we become his best friend. When we invest ourselves into the lives of others, their needs, their afflictions, their hopes and dreams become ours. Like the Good Samaritan, we involve ourselves, instead of crossing over to the other side of the road like the unsympathetic religious leaders.

Second, we see an urgent need. A fellow minister and I travelled through Turkey in a rental car across the route Paul often used, on our way to the ancient site of Lystra. We left Iconium, as the sun began to set and headed for a village called Hatunsaray. We knew from books that Lystra was nothing more than a mound, located a couple of miles from the little Turkish village, but we wanted to see the area anyway.

Our anxiety level grew as we saw the sun starting to slip behind the Pisidian hills. Finally, just before the sun completely disappeared, we made it to Hatunsaray—only to find a herd of sheep slowly making its way right down the main street in town. We reluctantly fell in line behind them, resigned to the fact that we were not going to see Lystra this night. As we crept along at a snail's pace, I noticed a local man standing beside the road. I tried asking him where Lystra was but he only looked quizzically at my attempts to communicate to him. "Lie-stra?" I asked. He shrugged. Finally, a cheerful look came upon his face as he exclaimed, "Lee-stra?"

"Yes! yes!" I exclaimed. Motioning to get in our car, he jumped in the back seat and led us to what remained of Lystra. We had flashlights but soon discovered there really was not much to see, after all. We drove back to the village, satisfied that we had done what we could to visit the site where Timothy grew up and where Paul was stoned.

When we returned to the village, the man invited us to join him for some tea. For the remainder of that evening the men of the village treated us like royalty. They fed us, gave us tea, and treated us like long, lost friends. We ended up spending the night in the home of one of the town's leading men.

In the Near Eastern culture, if a traveler shows up at your home, you do everything possible to make him feel welcomed. You feed him and give him a place to sleep. Once he arrives at your home his needs become your responsibility.

In the Jesus' story, the host understands his responsibility. The guest must be fed. but there is no food in the house. In great embarrassment, the host goes out into the city streets, determined to find food for his visitor.

Jesus' point is that there is a great urgency in filling the need. Jack Hayford brings this out:

> And Jesus said the reason the midnight seeker gets what he needs is because of his anaideia—not his reverence, not his modest sensitivity to the hour, not his caution, nor his respect for propriety, but his bold unashamedness—indeed, his brassiness.
>
> It isn't the brassiness of a smart aleck making demands but the forwardness of a person who is so taken with an awareness of need that he abandons normal protocol.[4]

Third, we see why he bangs on his neighbor's door with dogged persistence: his inability to meet the need himself. If he had food in the house, he would have had no reason to ask. But since he cannot meet the needs with what he has at hand, he must go find someone who can.

Lacking the proper resources to meet others' needs drives us to prayer on their behalf. Sometimes we can help people with our own abilities and efforts. This is what we have seen in the two preceding chapters. But there are some needs we simply cannot meet on our own. We must go to the benevolent Judge who pities the person in need Himself.

The fourth thing is the host was willing to sacrifice to meet his guest's need. Do you think he was excited about getting out of bed to go bang on an inappreciative neighbor's door in the middle of the night? Of course not! He did it because the alternative of not meeting the need was not an option. One manifestation of a life of victory is when the needs of others outweigh one's own personal comforts and desires. What kind of Christianity would it be if a person never learns to put the needs of others before his own? Certainly it would be anything but victorious!

The fifth thing the story teaches is that he went to the door of a friend. A relationship had already been established.

When we seek God on behalf of another, we expect an answer because we know what He is like. He is compassionate, even if He does have to be awakened in the middle of the night. Just as in the case of our benevolent judge, it is important that we see the abundance in God's heart. We do not go to God looking for a few scraps of dried out, old bread, we go looking for a feast. God wants to pour out blessings. The right combination of need and requests allows Him to do so.

Lastly, we must see the importance of relentless banging on the door of the throne room. God is looking for those who will not be denied, who will not be turned away, who will not take no for an answer. He loves to hear that door banging! Notice what He tells the Jews through the prophet Isaiah:

> On your walls, O Jerusalem, I have appointed
> watchmen; all day and all night they will never keep

silent. You who remind the LORD, take no rest for
yourselves; and give Him no rest until He establishes
and makes Jerusalem a praise in the earth. (Isaiah 62:7)

We must stop thinking that God has to be convinced to do
good. Something as precious as a soul will not be won easily. A very
real war goes on for that soul. It takes much prayer to appropriate
God's need-filling mercies into the person's life. Every time we
pray, God answers.

The Prayer of Mercy

I have learned a prayer that can be a help to those who wish
to uphold others in prayer and may be lacking the structure to do so.
"Lord, flood that one I am thinking about with need-filling mercies."[5]

We have seen how mercy is God's supply system to meet the
needs of people. Only God understands what is in a man's heart.
Only God knows the needs of a soul. We may see some problems and
think we know how to pray, but it is usually better to bring the person
to the throne of God and entrust the Lord with their needs. When we
pray that He will send mercies into someone's situation, we are
asking God to meet their needs as He sees them. Just like an
antibiotic goes through a person's system combating a virus, when
we pray this way, we are opening a floodgate of mercies to enter that
person's life. Those mercies will seek out and destroy anything that
is seeking to bring harm to the person's well being.

When praying for God's mercy and His blessing on someone's
life we align ourselves with the Lord. There are two persons before
the throne of God regarding us at any given time. The Bible tells us
that Satan is "the accuser of the brethren" (Revelation 12:10) and that
Jesus "lives to make intercession for" us (Hebrews 7:25; 9:24). The
reality of our words is that when we gossip, criticize, or put others
down, we curse them and operate in the spirit Satan is in. On the
other hand, when we encourage others, build them up, or intercede
on their behalf, we put ourselves in the Spirit that Jesus is in: the
Spirit of blessing. Two people before the throne. Two spirits we can
partake of.

As we pray for others, we want the Lord to bless them
abundantly. Remember the benevolent judge? We won't be content

with a light drizzle; we want an outpouring! We aren't going to go before the Throne looking for a trickle; we want floods. We are not thinking of a puddle of mercies for their needs, we are looking for an ocean. God is a God of abundance and that is the kind of answer we petition on behalf of our loved ones.

As our intercessory prayer life grows, we find ourselves praying for people we come into contact with throughout the day. "Lord, flood that grocery clerk with Your fulfilling mercies. Meet her needs as You see them." When we are tempted to get angry, we immediately begin praying, thus fulfilling the commandment of Jesus who said that we should "pray for those who mistreat" us (Luke 6:28). If a Christian man sees a scantily dressed girl, rather than trying to battle lust in his own strength, he can do mercy toward her through prayer, thus cleansing his heart (Luke 11:41). His inside world, which has been so accustomed to criticism, lust, anger, resentment, and envy, will gradually be transformed into a fountain of blessing.

The Need Of The Hour

Today's greatest need in the Body of Christ is for believers to know how to intercede for others. There is no mercy so great, no deed so selfless, and no act which can accomplish more for others than that of intercession. In spite of all the honor we give to national media figures in this country, there is no higher calling in the Christian Church than to that of intercessory prayer.

During some of the darkest days in the history of Israel, they had a problem finding those who would intercede. Isaiah said that the Lord "saw that there was no man, and was astonished that there was no one to intercede" (Isaiah 59:6). In Ezekiel, the Lord said, "And I searched for a man among them who should build up the wall and stand in the gap before Me for the land, that I should not destroy it; but I found no one" (Ezekiel 22:30).

How tragic! The vivid images in Lamentations of mothers cooking their own babies and wholesale slaughter by the Babylonians gives you an idea of the repercussions of that lack. Do we in America face the same kind of devastation because God cannot find those willing to stand in the gap for those in need? Possibly so.

Here's what Andrew Murray said about God's search for intercessors:

God seeks intercessors. There is a world with its perishing millions, with intercession as its only hope. So much love and work are comparatively vain, because there is so little intercession. There are millions living as if there had never been a Son of God to die for them. Every year, millions pass into the outer darkness without hope. Millions bear the Christian name, but the great majority of them live in utter ignorance or indifference. Millions of feeble, sickly Christians, thousands of wearied workers, could be blessed by intercession, could help themselves to become mighty in intercession. Churches and missions sacrificing life and labor with little results often lack the power of intercession. Souls, each one worth more than worlds—worth nothing less than the price paid for them in Christ's blood—are within reach of the power that can be won by intercession. We surely have no conception of the magnitude of the work to be done by God's intercessors, or we would cry to God above everything to give us the spirit of intercession.

God seeks intercessors. There is a God of glory able to meet all these needs. We are told that He delights in mercy, that He waits to be gracious, that He longs to pour out His blessing. We are told that the love which gave the Son up to death is the same love that each moment hovers over every human being. And yet He does not help. And there they perish. It is as if God does not move. If He does so love and long to bless, there must be some inscrutable reason for His holding back. What can it be? Scripture says it is because of your unbelief. It is the faithlessness and consequent unfaithfulness of God's people. He has taken them up into partnership with Himself. He has honored them, and bound Himself, by making their prayers one of the standard measures of the working of His power. Lack of intercession is one of the chief reasons for the lack of blessing. O that we would turn our eyes and heart from everything else and fix them on this God who hears prayer. Let the magnificence of His promises, His power and His purpose of love overwhelm us![6]

Part Four
The Fruits of Living in Victory

Meditation For Today

"War is an ugly thing, but not the ugliest thing: the decayed and degrading state of moral and patriotic feeling which thinks that nothing is worth a war is worse... A man who has nothing for which he is willing to fight, nothing which he cares about more than his personal safety, is a miserable creature who has no chance of being free, unless made and kept so by the exertions of better men than himself."[1]

John Stuart Mill

"Do you really want to see divine power at work? Then discard your human notions of power and look at the way Christ lived and died."[2]

Edmund A. Steimle

"The Holy Spirit is God resident on earth. All divine power resides in Him. He is looking for those who are honest enough to be trusted with the power He can give them. They alone will use it for God's glory and not for themselves."[3]

Gordon Chilvers

"Satan laughs at our toiling, mocks at our wisdom, but trembles when we pray."[4]

Unknown Author

Chapter Fifteen

Walking in Spiritual Authority

Spiritual warfare has become quite a sensation in the American Church. Prayer groups meet in our churches where part of the corporate prayer time is spent "pulling down strongholds." Macho saints at spiritual warfare conferences go around karate chopping imaginary demons. Believers in deliverance churches sometimes writhe on the floor, screaming, and retching as others "cast demons out of them." Groups go out to the red-light districts and march around bars and porn shops "taking authority" over the ruling devils there. Others spend the bulk of their prayer times talking to demons, roaring like lions, binding and loosing, renouncing and breaking generational curses.

Why are some believers so exhilarated with the idea of conquering the devil? Perhaps it gives them a sense of power when bullying a demon around or better yet, when they're instrumental in the pulling down of some monstrous principality over a city. But with all of this warfare going on, one might wonder why things never seem to get any better.

Spiritual Warfare

War is a struggle or conflict between opposing groups, each trying to overcome the other through the use of force. Military commanders use strategy, planning, moves, and counter moves. There is guerrilla warfare. There are huge, open battles. There are covert operations. There are quick strikes and lengthy campaigns. There are patrols that get in firefights and there are spies who gather intelligence. There are naval skirmishes, air battles, missile strikes, and hand-to-hand combat. These are all elements of 21st century warfare.

Spiritual warfare involves conflict between the forces of God, which would include believers, angels, and the power of the Holy Spirit, and the forces of Satan, which would include the unsaved and the devils they serve.

Some warriors mistake the battle to be between believers and unbelievers and presume they can win by legislating morality. They picket porn shops and abortion clinics. They petition senators and representatives. They write books, appear on television, and speak on radio. They try to win spiritual battles through political means.*

Other warriors, perhaps a little closer to the reality of the situation, make it a warfare which solely exists between angels and demons. They imagine that there are heavenly warriors with shining swords standing guard over them. They imagine demons ready to pounce upon them at every turn. Battles are being fought in the skies as they go to work.

Neither of these groups is entirely wrong. However there is one element of this conflict that both groups seem to discount or overlook: the power of the Holy Spirit. We forget that there is a sovereign God reigning over the entire creation. He isn't absent, nor is He uninvolved. The following verses are among the many that show the extent of His involvement:

> The eyes of the LORD are toward the righteous, and His ears are open to their cry. The face of the LORD is against evildoers, to cut off the memory of them from the earth. The righteous cry and the LORD hears, and delivers them out of all their troubles. The

---

* I sincerely appreciate the efforts of Christian activists who are attempting to make America a better place to live. But this is a battle that must be won primarily on one's knees.

LORD is near to the brokenhearted, and saves those who are crushed in spirit. Many are the afflictions of the righteous; but the LORD delivers him out of them all (Psalms 34:15-19).

Charles Spurgeon observes:

> "The eyes of the Lord are upon the righteous." He observes them with approval and tender considerations; they are so dear to him that he cannot take his eyes off them; he watches each one of them as carefully and intently as if there were only that one creature in the universe.
> "His ears are open unto their cry." His eyes and ears are thus both turned by the Lord towards his saints; his whole mind is occupied about them: if slighted by all others, they are not neglected by him. Their cry he hears at once, even as a mother is sure to hear her sick babe; the cry may be broken, plaintive, unhappy, feeble, unbelieving, yet the Father's quick ear catches each note of lament or appeal, and he is not slow to answer his children's voice.[5]

I do not discount the power given to the devil in this world. His influence and power are very real. I also do not want to minimize the involvement of angels in the affairs of men—especially believers. The Bible clearly teaches us that they help us and fend for us spiritually. But most importantly, let's keep in mind that overshadowing all of this is the presence of the Almighty.

Anatomy Of A Spiritual Defeat

The following story describes one of my greatest failures since becoming a Christian. In 1993, Kathy and I spent several weeks during the Christmas season in Jerusalem with friends of ours who minister there. Our friend suggested that if we wished to see Bethlehem, located in the West Bank, that we might want to take advantage of the festivities being held there on Christmas Eve by the Catholic Church. "There will be thousands of tourists there. It will be safe for you."

With that assurance, we got on one of the special buses provided for the occasion and took the short ride down to Bethlehem. There weren't many tourists on our bus, but we assumed it was because we were going early in the day. The bus pulled up to the checkpoint, and a soldier quickly jumped aboard and looked around, got off, and waved us through. We had entered the West Bank.

When we arrived in Bethlehem, we were escorted up to Manger Square (the scene of recent gun battles) and were released to enter the enclosed area on our own. A group of soldiers, each armed with an Uzi, stood at each street approaching the plaza. Crowds of Palestinians lined up at each checkpoint, receiving a cursory search before being allowed to enter. Tension was thick as the hated Israeli soldiers warily kept an eye out for possible terrorists attacks.

The Church of the Nativity dominated one side of Manger Square, with tourist shops lining the other three. Kathy and I visited some of the shops, as more and more people poured into the confined area. Tired of walking, we eventually settled into one of the outdoor cafes and ordered a cup of coffee. Once seated, we became the target of Palestinian kids who converged upon us with their candy bars and trinkets they wished to sell.

I really did feel bad for them and agreed to buy an unwanted candy bar from one of the more aggressive boys. I was surprised to discover that, rather than having the desired effect of sending them away, my purchase only spurred the others on to more aggressive behavior. Kathy and I honestly tried to show those children Jesus. We smiled sweetly at them and apologized that we couldn't afford to buy anything else from them. At that, one of them opened a packet of sugar and dumped it all over my camera which was sitting on the table.

We continued to stay in the right spirit in spite of their rudeness, but we gradually began to feel on edge. Finally, we realized that sitting there seemed to urge them on, so we decided to go for a walk. We had seen all of the shops and didn't care to see the Church of the Nativity. We decided to head back to the parking lot where buses arrived and departed. Before we got far, a little girl accosted us and demanded that we buy one of her candy bars. We kept saying that we didn't want one. Finally, with the face of the devil himself, she slammed the candy bar into Kathy's chest, trying to make her take it. We finally got away from her.

While all of this was going on with these kids, we hadn't noticed that the Square had filled up with thousands of people—not the throngs of tourists we had expected—but Palestinians. There was spiritual warfare there that day. Most of those people had a spirit of hatred for the Jewish people and were in a spiritual battle without realizing it. Had I been in a better state spiritually, I would have been more spiritually fit to engage in a small degree of my own warfare, but jet lag had produced sleepless nights and shortened prayer times which, in turn, brought about spiritual weakness in both of us.

Kathy and I were on the south side of the square, which was now packed wall to wall with people. To get to the bus we had to fight through this crowd to the other side. I plunged into the mostly male crowd and began elbowing my way through to the other side. About a third of the way through, I looked back and saw Kathy crying. "Can we go back? I just want to go back!" she pleaded. Puzzled about what in the world could be wrong with her, I agreed. Once we got out of the mob, she told me that a number of men had groped her while we were in the crowd.

At this, all of the frustration of dealing with those kids welled up in me, and I became enraged. I wanted to kill a Palestinian. Although I had no idea which ones had assaulted my wife, I was content to lay hands on any one of them I could. I couldn't get myself to just attack an innocent person chosen at random, so I entertained the thought of provoking a fight.

I began walking through the crowd, glaring at the men, pushing some out of my way. If I would have had my way that day, the CNN cameras filming the whole scene would have probably gotten some great footage of an American tourist being stomped to death by an angry mob. With adrenalin rushing through my veins, I had no fear of those Palestinians. Even though I was in the wrong spirit, sensing God's hand on my life gave me added confidence. God did have His hand on my life and kept me from making a fatal error.

Eventually, a soldier agreed to take us through the crowd and after several miserable hours there, we escaped without harm—physically that is. I hadn't given myself over to wrath like that since my days in the sheriff's department. It would have been one thing if I would have gotten violent in the protection of my wife, but that wasn't the case. The assault had already happened, and I was just out for revenge.*

The Holy Spirit

Jesus was in a different Spirit while He walked those Judean streets. He had enemies who sought to harm Him, and yet He responded with gentleness and in love. His enemies lived in a spirit of murder toward Him. He could have responded like I did or like James and John did on one occasion. When a town of Samaritans rejected Jesus and the disciples, James and John wanted to bring fire down from heaven. Jesus rebuked them saying, "You do not know what kind of spirit you are of; for the Son of Man did not come to destroy men's lives, but to save them" (Luke 9:56).

Peter also wanted to fight in the flesh. When the mob came to arrest Jesus in the Garden of Gethsemane, he lopped off a man's ear with his sword. Jesus immediately healed the man saying, "Put your sword back into its place; for all those who take up the sword shall perish by the sword. Or do you think that I cannot appeal to My Father, and He will at once put at My disposal more than twelve legions of angels?" (Matthew 26:53).

When it comes to spiritual warfare, you do not fight fire with fire. The devil will incite people against you. Sometimes the devil will attempt to incite you against others. The spirit you are in determines how well you do spiritually. You can claim to be a warrior for Christ, but the efficacy of your warfare depends upon the way you live your life.

Spiritual Authority

Matthew tells us that after Jesus finished the revolutionary Sermon on the Mount, the people were amazed because "He was teaching them as one having authority, and not as their scribes" (Matthew 7:28-29).

---

*I spent much time in repentance over this ugly incident. A few years later the Lord allowed me to "make it up," when I was given the opportunity to minister to Palestinians in a number of meetings in Amman, Jordan.

What gave Jesus such spiritual authority that the scribes did not have? Obviously He was the Son of the Living God and had authority for that reason alone. But there is something more which points to the authority that we too can enjoy as believers.

In Matthew 5-7, Jesus is speaking His mind to the multitude assembled. Hundreds of books have been written and thousands of sermons preached on the principles presented in those three short chapters. These glorious truths of God along with "the love chapter" (I Corinthians 13) represent the Spirit that Jesus always lived in. He spoke with and had authority because He lived in the reality of those words in His daily life.

Authority comes from a source of power, not words. If I am walking down the street and someone yells at me to stop, it doesn't matter how loudly he screams, with what authority he yells or what he looks like. I might think, *Who does he think he is?* If, however, he is wearing a uniform with a badge on it, I am suddenly very attentive. The authority comes from who he represents, namely the government of the United States of America.

Jesus perfectly represented God because He walked in absolute submission to God. His authority was established by His obedience to the Father. The apostle Paul also had tremendous spiritual authority. He knew what it meant to battle with the powers of darkness. He wasn't running around throwing karate chops at imaginary demons! In Ephesians 6 he said:

> Finally, be strong in the Lord, and in the strength of His might. Put on the full armor of God, that you may be able to stand firm against the schemes of the devil. For our struggle is not against flesh and blood, but against the rulers, against the powers, against the world forces of this darkness, against the spiritual forces of wickedness in the heavenly places (Ephesians 6:10-12).

First, Paul addresses the fact that our strength comes from the power of God. We know that, but many of us do not understand how to appropriate this power. The believer is invested with the power and authority of God to the very degree that he is filled with His

Spirit and does His will.

The police officer's authority goes only as far as the power granted him by the State. He has the right to stop me as I walk down the street if it is in connection with a crime committed or the safety of the public. He does not have the right to stop me simply because he wants to impress his girlfriend with how much authority he has. If he stops me with that motivation, he can be fired from his job and possibly even arrested. His authority is by no means limitless—He too must stay within certain bounds.

As the Lord leads and empowers, believers have authority over devils. The empowering comes through being in the Spirit of Mercy, laying down our lives to meet the needs of others. The person who is being driven by this Spirit has tremendous authority with demons. Such spiritual authority is the irresistible power of God being manifested in his life.

We see this very principle at work in Paul's life in Ephesus. Luke tells us that "God was performing extraordinary miracles by the hands of Paul, so that handkerchiefs or aprons were even carried from his body to the sick, and the diseases left them and the evil spirits went out" (Acts 19:11-12).

Can you imagine having that kind of power over diseases and devils? This level of authority comes from living in the will of God. God's will is to meet the needs of other people: to love them. Paul's entire life revolved around the needs of others. God used him because he learned the secret of being an empty vessel which could be filled with the power of the Almighty—to do His will.

Do I believe in deliverance? Absolutely! Jesus set people free from evil spirits. Paul cast demons out of people. We can do it today, too, but first we must have an infilling of the Spirit that gives us that kind of authority over those devils. However, it should be noted that these two didn't hold special deliverance services or spiritual warfare conferences. Totally surrendered to God's will, they simply went about doing deeds of mercy, which sometimes included casting devils out of those oppressed.

Unfortunately, many believers want the power without the sacrifice. They want to feel like mighty men or women of God who can command the devils of hell to obey them. They are more interested in how it makes them look or feel than in the well-being of those in need. They imagine themselves in a place of authority that simply doesn't exist. They think that the name of Jesus gives them carte blanche in the spirit realm and devils have to obey their every word. But it doesn't work that way.

While in Ephesus, Paul encountered some religious Jews anxious to cast out demons. However, compassion didn't motivate them. They were professional magicians seeking to profit from their sorcery. One day, they approached a devil-possessed man and having seen the results of miracles performed by Paul, tried to use the name of Jesus.

"I adjure you by Jesus whom Paul preaches," they said, ordering the demon out of the man. The evil spirit answered them, "I recognize Jesus, and I know about Paul, but who are you?" Luke goes on to tell us that the man, filled with the strength of the devil, overpowered them and gave them such a beating that they fled naked (Acts 19:13-16).

The Real Battle

Before engaging in spiritual warfare, we must decide first and foremost, whose will are we going to obey. Paul tells us to put on the armor of God for a reason—that we will stand firm against the schemes of the devil.

Demons constantly scheme to get us to be in the spirit that they are in. We are tempted to lie, to lust, to cheat, to steal, to rise up in anger or pride. The Lord gently tries to get us to be in the Spirit that He is in. The real battle is over which will we will obey. Unfortunately, most believers obey the devil far more than they realize.

When Christians argue over biblical doctrine, do you think God's will or the devil's is being done? When a mother puts her kids in front of a television set for hour on end, whose will is being accomplished? When a man gets angry on the way to work because someone cuts him off in traffic, which spirit is he in? When an evangelist shows up in front of a crowd of well-wishers in a spirit of self-importance, whom is he emulating? When a couple drives by the destitute without any compassion for their plight, what spirit are they in? These examples represent the rule, not the exception in the American Church.

The real battle going on over your life at all times revolves around your will. Will you do mercy to others or continue to harden your heart against their needs? Will you allow God to humble you, or will you remain high-minded and prideful? Will you devote yourself to others, or will you continue in your selfishness? Will you obey Him from your heart, or will you continue on in self-will?

The tragedy is that we have weakened our position by "sleeping with the enemy." Sluggish and full of compromise, we have no authority left when we need it. The devils are mocking our words and laughing at our conferences. I can imagine how demons respond when believers come together in one of their spiritual warfare conferences. Perhaps it would sound something like this:

"Do you think I'm going to listen to you, Phil? You just snapped at your kids in your big rush to get to the conference! Yeah, right!"

"Who are you talking to, Sue? I was just with you on your tenth spending spree of the month down at the mall! You listened to my promptings the whole time!"

"Who do you think you are, Jim? I was watching you undress that girl in your mind on the way over here! I'm sure you're going to bind me! Ha, ha, ha!"

Can we obey the voice of a demon one minute and the next cast him out of somebody? The reason Paul walked in such authority over devils is that they had no hold on him. He was utterly given over to the Spirit of the Lord. If you surrender to God in this way, devils will be running out screaming when you speak! They cannot stand against someone who obeys Jesus from the heart. Until you take your walk with God seriously, don't expect the devils of hell to take your words seriously.

The believer who lives in the words of Jesus, such as those given in the Sermon on the Mount, will have the power of God in his life and will hold authority over every devil he encounters. *The victory he wins over his own rebellious nature allows him to be victorious over the enemy.* The size of the ministry, number of stations that carry a radio preacher, or the amount of money coming in daily means nothing to the foul spirits of hell. If that were the case the Mormons would hold tremendous spiritual power. Show me one believer who quietly lives the love of God described in Chapter 12 of this book, and I will show you someone that leaves the devils of hell shaking. This precious saint will never hear, "I recognize Jesus, and I know about Paul, but who are you?"

Meditation For Today

"I do not blame ungodly men for rushing to their pleasures. Let them have their fill. That is all they have to enjoy, but Christians must seek their delights in a higher sphere than the insipid frivolities of the world. Vain pursuits are dangerous to renewed souls...

"It is the sweetness of sin that makes it the more dangerous. Satan never sells his poisons naked; he always gilds them before he vends them. Beware of pleasures... It is said that where the most beautiful cacti grow, there the most venomous serpents lurk. It is so with sin. Your fairest pleasures will harbor your grossest sins. Take care!"[1]

C. H. Spurgeon

"By lovingkindness and truth iniquity is atoned for, and by the fear of the Lord one keeps away from evil."[2]

Solomon

"If sin rules in me, the life of God will be killed in me; if God rules in me, sin will be killed in me. There is no possible ultimate but that."[3]

Oswald Chambers

"True triumphs are God's triumphs over us. His defeats of us are our real victories."[4]

Henry Alford

Chapter Sixteen

Victory Over Habitual Sin

In the early '60s, six WEC missionaries ran a radio station in a dangerous area of the Congo. The sunbeam of the group was a young bachelor named Bill McChesney or "Smiling Bill," as everyone called him. Although only 5 foot 2 inches tall and 110 pounds, he made up for his size with exuberance.

The Congo during this time was tense with strife. The Simbas, a tribe rebellious to the white rule in Africa, were attacking and killing people all around the area. They repeatedly put the missionaries at the little compound through terrifying trial runs of coming to kill them, only to leave without harming them at all.

On November 14, 1964, they came and took little Bill McChesney away, even though he was ill with malaria. Also held captive were four missionaries from another compound. One of them, James Rodger, was the opposite to the effervescent Smiling Bill in every way. Though solemn and staid, his love for the Lord was unquestionable. During their ten days together in captivity the two became dear friends.

One day an arriving rebel officer turned livid when he saw Bill McChesney. "Why is the man still free?" he demanded. "Take him to prison at once!" When Bill was pushed into a truck, Jim

Rodger jumped in to accompany his new friend. During the trip, the soldiers beat Bill mercilessly. Already weakened by the malaria, the little guy couldn't stand under the attack and upon arriving, Jim had to carry him into the prison.

The next morning a colonel arrived and demanded to know their nationalities. Bill acknowledged being American, and Jim, British. Upon hearing this the colonel was about to have Bill killed, but Jim stood next to him saying, "If you must die, brother, I'll die with you."

The colonel motioned for the mob of rebels to attack them. They came at them swinging clubs and fists. Bill was killed quickly. Jim caught him and gently laid him on the ground. The mob then knocked him down and kicked and trampled him to death also.

Multiply this story by millions, and you will have a fairly accurate impression of what it has meant to serve Christ down through the centuries. It's not those who are being persecuted around the world today who are the oddballs, it is the modern American Christian who lives for SELF. He is the one who is out of synch with the heritage of the true Church of Jesus Christ.

Our Savior was crucified, 11 of the 12 disciples were martyred, and Paul the Apostle was beheaded. This established the way it would be for most of the next 19 centuries; and if not martyrdom, persecution; and if not persecution, deprivation; and if not deprivation, sacrificial service to others. This has been the glory of the Body of Christ throughout its history.

Unfortunately, this cannot be said of the 21st century American Church. In fact, we have drifted so far off course spiritually that one of our chief characteristics today is our focus on *self*-help. At a time when the Christian Church should be battling the forces of hell in preparation for the great conflict over the Second Coming of Christ, we are so bogged down with personal problems and addictions that we can't even get in the ring!

How can this be? The answer is that as a society we have become extremely selfish. Most of us have been born into the "me generation." We have been taught to see ourselves as the center of everything: what *I* want, where *I* want to go, what makes *me* feel good, what fulfills *me*. Even the Christian faith, which should motivate us into a selfless concern for the needs of others, is viewed as one more source of getting something for self. The sheer number of books available today about what God wants to do for the individual Christian is evidence of a distorted view of Christianity.

What a contrast to Paul's life! His statements show his perspectives on the Christian faith as compared to that of the majority of professing Christians today:

> Therefore also we have as our ambition, whether at home or absent, to be pleasing to Him. For we must all appear before the judgment seat of Christ, that each one may be recompensed for his deeds in the body, according to what he has done, whether good or bad.
>
> For the love of Christ controls us, having concluded this, that one died for all, therefore all died; and He died for all, that they who live should no longer live for themselves, but for Him who died and rose again on their behalf.
>
> Therefore if any man is in Christ, he is a new creature; the old things passed away; behold, new things have come (II Corinthians 5:9-17).
>
> Now we who are strong ought to bear the weaknesses of those without strength and not just please ourselves. Let each of us please his neighbor for his good, to his edification. For even Christ did not please Himself. (Romans 15:1-3)

Living Mercy To Others

Addiction is the outcome of a selfish desire for some particular pleasure. It stands to reason then that selflessness counters compulsive, selfish desires in a person's heart.

The root of sin is coveting lust—wanting something for self. This passion drives people to commit sin. Satan uses it to inflame our lives. The lust for pleasure, gain, position, power over others, and a host of other evils form a foundation for those bound up in various addictions.

Fortunately, God also has a passion. His passion is to do good to others, to help others, to meet needs. It is *agape*—unconditional love—which manifests itself through acts of mercy. It can be a root in our lives as well as a foundation. As we saw in Chapter 12, this desire to do good forms a basis of godliness that the Lord uses to build ministry upon.

God's ardent desire to meet needs is the only thing that can utterly root out and defeat the passion for sin. As long as *self* rules a man's heart, he will never be truly free. As a person gets out of himself and sees the needs of those around him, a transformation begins to occur. His problems, which once seemed like an insurmountable mountain, diminish in the light of other's needs. The more he focuses upon himself—what he wants and thinks he needs—the stronger sin is in his life.

It isn't enough, however, just to *see* needs; we must *do* something about those needs. In the process of doing mercy, the heart is changed. I can remember many times that I was discouraged (or even depressed) only to find myself thrust into a counseling situation where I was forced to get out of my own problems to help others. I cannot think of one single instance that serving others didn't immediately pull me out of my gloom.

Intercession Changes The Heart

Interceding for the needs of others is the greatest mercy we can do for each other. Doing mercy is, of course, a very wonderful thing. However, there is a danger of slipping into a routine of doing good deeds to be noticed by others—again, more self! If the motivation of the heart isn't right, your best efforts for others accomplish nothing for your own personal needs. Paul stated:

> If I speak with the tongues of men and of angels, but do not have love, I have become a noisy gong or a clanging cymbal. And if I have the gift of prophecy, and know all mysteries and all knowledge; and if I have all faith, so as to remove mountains, but do not have love, I am nothing. And if I give all my possessions to feed the poor, and if I deliver my body to be burned, but do not have love, it profits me nothing (I Corinthians 13:1-3).

Here Paul shows us the futility of doing outward deeds—even those which would be considered deeds of mercy—without the inside motivation of doing it for the good of others.

When a man is dealing with habitual sin in his own life, he will overcome that sin as he begins to take the needs of others into his heart. Jesus tried to help the hard-hearted Pharisees find the inner cleansing they so desperately needed. He told them, "Now you Pharisees clean the outside of the cup and of the platter, but inside of you, you are full of robbery and wickedness. You foolish ones, did not He who made the outside make the inside also? But give that which is within as charity, and then all things are clean for you" (Luke 11:39-41).

Their inside world was full of sin. What could they do? Jesus gave them the way out. If they would do mercy in their hearts, something would change inside them—guaranteed. Jesus once said that the evil that comes out of a man's heart defiles him. If evil is in his heart, where is the best place to deal with it? In the heart, of course!

As we take the needs and burdens of others into our hearts, we become transformed, "cleansed." What a wonderful thing! The Lord gives us a way to cleanse our own hearts—by doing acts of mercy toward others inside our hearts.

A Case In Point

Len House* joined the staff of Pure Life Ministries as a counselor in January of 1996. We asked him to join us because he was willing to do whatever it took to find God and total victory over sin.

Len was a 20-year veteran of the Air Force. He spent 10 years as a member of the elite para-rescue team trained to infiltrate enemy lines to find and rescue downed pilots. For more than seven years he was stationed in Korea where he became addicted to visiting prostitutes. This opened the door for great evil to enter his soul. An infatuation with sado-masochism slowly crept into his heart. Although he never acted it out with people, the fascination grew inside him.

---

* a pseudonym

Len spent his last several years in the Air Force stationed stateside. As his heart grew darker, he increasingly isolated himself from others. He was obsessed with force, power, and the control over other people. Len was an avid weight lifter, and was actually obsessed with his physique. He once remarked that he would have made a great Nazi because his heart was brutal, and he gravitated to anything that allowed him to rule over others.

Through the quiet witness of a Christian captain, Len came to the Lord in 1993. His problems, of course, were still there, but at least he was seeing a way out. Although he heard about Pure Life Ministries in April of 1994, it took nine months before he was willing to come to the residential program for help with his sexual addictions.

Two things precipitated his decision. First, he was diagnosed with having osteoporosis, a degenerative bone disease. This was devastating to Len, who had always received so much of his self-worth from his physical strength. God was bringing him to his knees. Secondly, he began having horrible nightmares. A number of times he woke up feeling an evil presence in the room. One night, he woke up loudly cursing in a deep, guttural voice that wasn't his own. This terrified him.

In some ways, Len was a tough case for our counselors. The one thing that always stood out about him was his willingness to fight through and do whatever it took to gain victory over his sin. He had a lot of darkness to come out of, but gradually, he began to change. The principle Len latched onto that probably helped him more than any other thing was praying for others.

"I had always been told to turn to the Lord in my struggles, but I didn't really know what that meant," Len confides. "I prayed for myself, and it did seem to help, but I still felt stuck. When I started interceding for others—praying for God's mercy to meet their needs—everything began to come together for me. It was something concrete and practical I could do. At first, I didn't understand how it could help me, but my counselor told me to do it so I did.

"One thing I can see that has come out of it has

been the change in my attitude toward people. I used to hate people, women particularly, but the Lord is helping me to care about them as human beings.

"For instance, I used to be real self-righteous toward unsaved people, especially liberals or humanists, but I'm starting to have a heart for them. I can feel God's compassion for them in my heart."

Len House is a tremendous testimony of God's goodness coming into the life of a man willing to consider the needs of others. The same thing can happen to you. Those too proud to ask, too selfish to help others, and too hardhearted to believe in God's goodness will never change. They will stay in their rut of selfishness and sin will continue to enjoy dominion over their lives.

The person who struggles with sin will find the victory he is searching for when he starts living in an awareness of the needs around him and begins to give out the mercy to others that has been lavished upon him. Having a servant's heart will absolutely undermine the self-centered life and counteract the powerful temptation of lust for more ___*(fill in the blank)*___. Then, to his amazement—as well as others—a fundamental change will take place within him. Sin will no longer have control of his life.

Meditation For Today

"O soul, He only who created thee can satisfy thee. If thou ask for anything else, it is thy misfortune, for He alone who made thee in His image can satisfy thee."[1]

Augustine

"If (His presence) is all that God gives me, I am satisfied, but if all that He gave me was the (whole) world, I would not be satisfied."[2]

Jeremiah Burroughs

I Asked God
I asked God for strength, that I might achieve.
I was made weak, that I might learn to obey.
I asked for health, that I might do more things.
I was given infirmity, that I might do better things.
I asked for riches, that I might be happy.
I was given poverty, that I might be wise.
I asked for power, that I might have the praise of men.
I was given weakness, that I might feel the need of God.
I asked for all things, that I might enjoy life.
I was given life, that I might enjoy all things.
I got nothing that I asked for—but everything I had hoped for.
Almost despite myself, my unspoken prayers were answered.
I am, among all men, most richly blessed.[3]

Anonymous

Chapter Seventeen

Living In Victory

Solomon's life is a tragic example to believers today about the price of sin. By the end of his life, however, Solomon had gained profound insights into some of the deepest revelations available about enjoying a victorious spiritual life.

David was 50 years old when Solomon was born to Bathsheba. David had already defeated all of his enemies. He had been king for 20 years, reigning 13 of those years in Jerusalem. David's life had been a paradox. At one time, he was a devout worshipper of God, but the carnal lifestyle of being the king of the land had taken its toll on his spiritual life. His lowest moment came when he committed adultery with Bathsheba and had her husband killed. David never fully recovered spiritually from this sin.

The only life Solomon knew as a young boy was one of security and prosperity. Probably more than any other figure in the Bible, his life was was quite similar to that of American believers today. He was taught the wonderful old stories of Abraham and Isaac, Jacob and Joseph, Moses and Pharaoh, Samson and Delilah. As a young boy his mother told him about the exploits of his great father—how he had killed a lion and a bear, his battle with Goliath, his skirmishes with the Philistines and his conflicts with Saul. Solomon was well versed in the Scriptures and knew the Psalms his father had penned, much like our children know the classic hymns we sing.

Solomon was also brought up without much discipline. We are told in 1 Kings 1:6 that David never crossed the will of his oldest son, Adonijah. We have no reason to believe that anything was different with his favorite, younger son. Nevertheless, by the time Solomon inherited the kingdom from his dying father, we are told that he "loved the Lord."

Pleased by this, God appeared to him in a dream and asked what He could do for him.

Solomon replied,

> Thou hast shown great lovingkindness to Thy servant David my father, according as he walked before Thee in truth and righteousness and uprightness of heart toward Thee; and Thou hast reserved for him this great lovingkindness, that Thou hast given him a son to sit on his throne, as it is this day. And now, O LORD my God, Thou hast made Thy servant king in place of my father David, yet I am but a little child; I do not know how to go out or come in. And Thy servant is in the midst of Thy people which Thou hast chosen, a great people who cannot be numbered or counted for multitude. So give Thy servant an understanding heart to judge Thy people to discern between good and evil. For who is able to judge this great people of Thine? (I Kings 3:6-9).

What an incredible display of poverty of spirit and selflessness! Solomon had a sincere desire to rule the people of God in the right way. He saw that he lacked the wisdom to lead Israel so he appealed to the lovingkindness (*hhesed*) of the Lord and asked for help.

This pleased the Lord immensely!

> "Because you have asked this thing and have not asked for yourself long life, nor have asked riches for yourself, nor have you asked for the life of your enemies, but have asked for yourself discernment to understand justice, behold, I have done according to your words.

Behold, I have given you a wise and discerning heart, so that there has been no one like you before you, nor shall one like you arise after you. And I have also given you what you have not asked, both riches and honor, so that there will not be any among the kings like you all your days. And if you walk in My ways, keeping My statutes and commandments, as your father David walked, then I will prolong your days" (I Kings 3:11-14).

Out of the anointing granted him through this dialogue, Solomon designed and built the fabulous temple and wrote many of the Proverbs.

It seemed that Solomon could do no wrong. Everything he touched turned to gold. When the Queen of Sheba traveled 1,200 miles to meet him, she went away stunned by the awesome display of riches and wisdom Solomon exhibited. These were her parting words to him:

It was a true report which I heard in my own land about your words and your wisdom. Nevertheless I did not believe the reports, until I came and my eyes had seen it. And behold, the half was not told me. You exceed in wisdom and prosperity the report which I heard. How blessed are your men, how blessed are these your servants who stand before you continually and hear your wisdom. Blessed be the LORD your God who delighted in you to set you on the throne of Israel; because the LORD loved Israel forever, therefore He made you king, to do justice and righteousness (I Kings 10:6-9).

Everything was going so wonderfully for the young king, and yet, within 30 years he became a miserable and empty old man. He later said that he came to the place where he actually "hated life" (Ecclesiastes 2:17).* Before it was all over, the king who had once loved

---

* The Turner Broadcasting Company produced a video about his life that really captured the misery of his sin. Other than the unfortunate explicit "love scenes" with the Queen of Sheba, I highly recommend it.

the Lord turned from Him and built temples for demon worship. Even the most sincere beginning can have a tragic ending if a man doesn't keep his focus on the Lord.

What happened to Solomon was what we all have secretly wished for at some point. He was given a free license to have all that his heart desired. We are told in the Book of Ecclesiastes that he tried to fill his life with knowledge (1:16), pleasure (2:1), laughter (2:2), building projects (2:4-6), slaves (2:7), flocks and herds (2:7), silver, gold, and treasures (2:8), entertainment (2:8), and finally, sexual pleasure (2:9). In fact, he says, "all that my eyes desired I did not refuse them. I did not withhold my heart from any pleasure..." (Ecclesiastes 2:10).

Doesn't this sound like the pursuit of the American dream? Recent statistics say much about the U. S. lifestyle. The living standard of the average welfare recipient in America ranks within the middle class of the other top 10 countries of the world; our poorest people live better than those of over 240 other nations. The second statistic states that the average American cat eats better than at least one billion people on our planet—people just like you and me!

In the U.S., we enjoy a more opulent lifestyle—full of luxury, pleasure, and comfort—than many kings down through world history. Solomon certainly didn't enjoy indoor plumbing, electricity, television, newspapers, toasters, automobiles, ambulance service, telephones, and all of the other things that we now consider absolute necessities. Yesterday's luxuries have become today's necessities. Recent examples include microwaves and personal computers. It wasn't that long ago that only the rich could afford such commodities. Now, most homes in America have both. Over the last 100 years we have increasingly raised our standard of living to the point now even our cats eat better than almost a third of the world's people.

This tremendous prosperity tends to keep people in a constant state of wanting more. Moreover, advertisers do a remarkable job of training us to never be satisfied. Everywhere we look we are being told about some new item that we just *cannot* live without. Clothes, computers, cars, vacations, houses, and furniture are paraded before us to keep us in a fixed state of covetousness. Always lusting for more, we are never satisfied.

Solomon was able to achieve every carnal dream and in the end, saw it all for what it was. "Thus I considered all my activities which my hands had done and the labor which I had exerted, and behold all was vanity and striving after wind and there was no profit under the sun" (Ecclesiastes 2:11). He came to see the futility and emptiness of chasing the pleasures of this world. "Vanity of vanities," he lamented, "all is vanity!" (Ecclesiastes 1:2). If the things of this world aren't yet empty to you, your mind is still being successfully manipulated by the voice of this world.

Jonah learned this hard lesson when he tried going his own way in rebellion to the call of God on his life. "Those who pay regard to false, useless and worthless idols forsake their own mercy and lovingkindness" (Jonah 2:8 Amplified Bible). When the pursuit of pleasure and material possessions become your focus in life, a victorious life in God is impossible and emptiness is sure to consume your heart.

When Solomon wrote Proverbs, he still believed he could handle riches and remain faithful to the Lord. It is interesting that it was Agur, not Solomon, who spoke this prayer in Proverbs 30: "...Give me neither poverty nor riches; feed me with the food that is my portion, lest I be full and deny Thee and say, 'Who is the LORD?...'" (Proverbs 30:8-9).

Agur's contentment is one of the key ingredients for a life of victory. Paul, sharing one of the principles of his life in Christ stated, "Not that I speak from want; for I have learned to be content in whatever circumstances I am. I know how to get along with humble means, and I also know how to live in prosperity; in any and every circumstance I have learned the secret of being filled and going hungry, both of having abundance and suffering need" (Philippians 4:11-12).

It is very important to remain content with the circumstances we have in life. Left to our own, we would go the way of Solomon, convinced that we could still remain faithful to God. Aren't you glad God doesn't let you ruin your life like Solomon did?

While contentment is important, it will not bring victory by itself.

Living In Gratitude

An ungrateful person is the most miserable of all people. He spent his life continually striving for a higher position, more things, and more experiences. The subtle message behind this lifestyle is that when we get that next promotion or new house or whatever it is that compels us at the present time, we will somehow achieve happiness. But circumstantial happiness is temporary and elusive at best.

Our problem is that we simply do not realize how rich we are. Many men go through life pursuing things that never satisfy and missing those that can. New cars and large houses are not evil or bad in themselves, but do not afford a person true fulfillment or contentment. If we could ask Marilyn Monroe, Jimi Hendrix, Janice Joplin, John Belushi, and countless others who reached the pinnacle of success in this world, they could tell us about the emptiness they discovered there.

We Christians are often like the dirt farmers in Oklahoma. Most spent their entire lives trying to eke out a living when all they had to do was sink a pipe in the ground to the oil field located below, and they would have received fabulous riches. What I missed for much of my Christian life was what only a full heart in God can provide: joy and contentment. These are essential elements of victorious living.

One avenue to this victorious living is through the discipline of gratitude. An attitude of thankfulness is fostered as a person focuses on all that God provides. "Count your blessings, name them one by one," as the song goes. A practical way of doing this is to make a gratitude list. Once a week, take some aspect of your life— job, house, marriage, family, spiritual life,—and list 30, 40, or 50 things about it for which you are grateful. A Bible study on all that God gives the believer also develops a thankful heart. You might be surprised at how little exercises like these can change your perspective. God has already given us so much. Why should we keep ourselves locked into the miserable prison of dissatisfaction? A thankful heart will bring a life of joy and is one of the key elements to victory and yet it is not the most important one.

Fulfillment Of Obedience

Another vital aspect of the victorious Christian life is simple obedience. Fulfillment and happiness increase with daily obedience to God.

Suppose a college student has a major exam coming up tomorrow. Some friends come over and talk him into going out to a bar. He goes out and has a good time. The next morning he is tired and hung over. He hasn't studied like he should have and sure enough, he fails. Now he feels worse. His lack of self-discipline caused him to flunk this important test, bringing him dangerously close to failing the course altogether. This in turn affects his grade point average and subsequently his future. His confidence plummets. He feels more miserable than ever. For him life seems so empty and meaningless.

Those without hope remain trapped in a rut they can never seem to escape. When they suffer the inevitable fallout of their sin, they turn to the temporary thrill of sin for comfort. As Peter said, "It has happened to them according to the true proverb, 'A dog returns to its own vomit,' and, 'A sow, after washing, returns to wallowing in the mire" (II Peter 2:22). Such is the downward spiral of addictive living. Frequently, the misery of one failure has a domino effect, resulting in one after another. Then come the inevitable consequences of sin. It all spells D-E-F-E-A-T, doesn't it?

The wonderful thing about God's kingdom is that the same principles that work against a person can also work for him. Let's say that the teacher sits the student down and has a talk with him. "Jimmy, if you do well on this test, you can still pull out a C in this class. I want you to study hard!" When his friends come over that evening, he declines their invitation and stays home to study. He wakes up after a good night's sleep, rested and ready. He takes the test and not only passes it, but scores an A on it! This boosts his confidence and fills him with hope that maybe he *can* have a good career one day. So much often hinges on one decision.

Living in obedience to God's principles for life brings about a lifestyle of continual triumph. A person who lives a life of minimal obedience—he obeys only those commandments that are convenient—will never know real victory. His own rebellion minimizes the blessings that could be his. The song says it well: "Trust and obey, for there's no other way to be happy in Jesus, but to trust and obey."[4] Obedience provides another part of finding fulfillment in life, but it too, in itself, falls short of providing that fullness we all long for.

'Tis More Blessed

In the human scheme of things, there are two basic types of people: givers and takers. From the time I can remember, I was always a taker. I was completely selfish. Everything I did ultimately had something in it for me.

You would think that a person so consumed with achieving satisfaction would be the one who received the most satisfaction. But God's ways are not like ours. In this world, the one who seeks to take the most, receives the least.

The unsaved and worldly Christians alike try to find fulfillment in this world despite the superficial, fleeting happiness it offers. This is all that either of them has ever known. Neither have experienced real joy that comes from a life surrendered to God.

Happiness, however, is in its very essence a worldly concept. It is the sense of exhilaration one feels under favorable circumstances. If you go into a nightclub around ten o'clock in the evening, you will generally find extremely happy people. If you go to a stadium where the home team is winning, you will find happy people. If you go to the home of a young girl in love who has just been proposed to, you are going to find a happy person. Generally speaking, happiness is the feeling people have when things are going *their* way.

Find those partiers the next morning, or those fans when their team is losing, or the girl when the guy jilts her, and you will find a band of miserable creatures. Why? Their happiness was based upon their situation. Sadly, most Christians never know what it means to live above circumstances and experience the joy of the Lord no matter what happens in their lives.

Jesus knew another way of living. His wasn't a life of taking, but a life of giving. Even though He was rightly called "a man of sorrows," (Isaiah 53:3) because of the grief of dealing with unrepentant people, He was the most joyful person who ever walked this earth. Jesus was always giving and was always joyful. "It is more blessed to give than to receive," He said (Acts 20:35).

We can have that joy and fullness of life, too. As we learn to live the life of mercy to meet the needs of others, we will know real joy. But even living a life of giving will not, in itself, fill that great void in our hearts.

Our Greatest Need

Incorporating these different principles into his life keeps a man on the pathway into a life of victory. But no matter how well he does all of these things and more, he will never know the joy of an abundant life until he learns how to find it in God alone.

The Lord has revealed Himself to man through a number of names. Each name reveals something of His character, but most especially, something of how His character relates to man. There was one name He gave to Himself that really encompassed them all. In that eventful and dramatic moment when God appeared unto Moses in the burning bush, He called Himself, "I AM THAT I AM" (Exodus 3:14). Jesus also tapped into this name. Seven times in the Book of John, He used the name "I AM" to signify the different aspects of His provision for our need. "I am the bread of life... I am the light of the world... I am the door... I am the good shepherd... I am the resurrection and the life... I am the way, the truth and the life... I am the true vine" (John 6:35; 8:12; 10:7, 11; 11:25; 14:6; 15:1).

An excellent book on this subject, *We Would See Jesus* by Roy and Revel Hession, says the following:

> The special revelation which this name gives is that of the grace of God. "I am" is an unfinished sentence. It has no object. I am—what? What is our wonder when we discover, as we continue with our Bibles, that He is saying, "I AM whatever My people need" and that the sentence is only left blank that man may bring his many and various needs, as they arise, to complete it!
>
> Apart from human need this great name of God goes round and round in a closed circle, "I am that I am"—which means that God is incomprehensible. But the moment human need and misery present themselves, He becomes just what that person needs. The verb has at last an object, the sentence is complete and God is revealed and known. Do we lack peace? "I am thy peace," He says. Do we lack strength? "I am thy strength." Do we lack spiritual life? "I am thy life." Do we lack wisdom? "I am thy wisdom", and so on.
>
> The name "Jehovah" is really like a blank cheque. Your faith can fill in what He is to be to you— just what you need, as each need arises. It is not you,

moreover, who are beseeching Him for this privilege, but He who is pressing it upon you. He is asking you to ask. "Hitherto have ye asked nothing in My name: ask, and ye shall receive, that your joy may be full" (John 16:24). Just as water is ever seeking the lowest depths in order to fill them, so is Jehovah ever seeking out man's need in order to satisfy it. Where there is need, there is God. Where there is sorrow, misery, unhappiness, suffering, confusion, folly, oppression, there is the I AM, yearning to turn man's sorrow into bliss whenever man will let Him. It is not, therefore, the hungry seeking for bread, but the Bread seeking the hungry; not the sad seeking for joy, but rather Joy seeking the sad; not emptiness seeking fullness, but rather Fullness seeking emptiness. And it is not merely that He supplies our need, but He becomes Himself the fulfillment of our need. He is ever "I am that which My people need".[5]

This, of course, is a tremendous revelation, but how do we use this knowledge of God in our daily lives? Becoming filled by Him in such a way happens primarily through the process of seeking Him. As we seek the Great Provider, Jehovah Jireh shows up to fill our needs.

Much has already been stated in regards to seeking the Lord. However, seeking God is not simply one of the exercises we must incorporate into our lives. It is the road of Christianity and *the end of the road*. Everything written in this book is part of the whole picture, but inevitably it should all lead us back to the place where our hearts are longing to be in His presence.

David became a seeker after God. There was a time in his life when the Lord was truly his all in all. It is unfortunate that he lost much of what he had in God through prosperity and power. But we can still learn much from what he wrote during better times.

When Thou didst say, "Seek My face," my heart said to Thee, "Thy face, O LORD, I shall seek." Do not hide Thy face from me, do not turn Thy servant away in anger; Thou hast been my help; do not abandon me nor forsake me, O God of my salvation!" (Psalms 27:8).

> One thing I have asked from the LORD, that I shall seek: that I may dwell in the house of the LORD all the days of my life, to behold the beauty of the LORD, and to meditate in His temple (Psalms 27:4).

> O God, Thou art my God; I shall seek Thee earnestly; my soul thirsts for Thee, my flesh yearns for Thee, in a dry and weary land where there is no water. Thus I have beheld Thee in the sanctuary, to see Thy power and Thy glory. Because Thy lovingkindness is better than life, my lips will praise Thee. So I will bless Thee as long as I live; I will lift up my hands in Thy name. My soul is satisfied as with marrow and fatness, and my mouth offers praises with joyful lips (Psalms 63:1-5).

It isn't difficult to imagine the passion in David's voice, the joy in his heart, and his fulfillment in life when his eyes were fully fixed on the Lord. We must be careful not to imagine that these are the words of just another pious poem. They express the testimony of a real man who had a genuine encounter with the Living God which left him practically breathless. He was caught up with the beauty of God's holiness.

The wonderful thing is that you and I can have this same experience if we so desire. The choice is ever before us. Do we want the Lord in this all-encompassing way? Luke tells a story about two sisters who were given this very same choice:

> Now as they were traveling along, He entered a certain village; and a woman named Martha welcomed Him into her home. And she had a sister called Mary, who moreover was listening to the Lord's word, seated at His feet. But Martha was distracted with all her preparations; and she came up to Him, and said, "Lord, do You not care that my sister has left me to do all the serving alone? Then tell her to help me." But the Lord

answered and said to her, "Martha, Martha, you are worried and bothered about so many things; but only a few things are necessary, really only one, for Mary has chosen the good part, which shall not be taken away from her" (Luke 10:38-42).

It is interesting how individuals, even those with the same blood line and identical upbringing, can respond so differently to the Lord. He was in their house. He spoke words of life. One sat mesmerized, unable to move, beholding the same beauty that David saw. The other was distracted, worried, and bothered.

This incident points to one of the greatest problems we have in the Church today. Many who are attempting to feed others are too busy to take the time to be fed themselves, and thus, have nothing more to offer than a platter of old, stale bread. Living the mercy life can be overwhelming and demanding, but if we teach others, we must sit at the feet of Jesus! If we don't, we have nothing of value to give to others and will eventually burn out due to spiritual starvation.

Jesus described Mary's experience of sitting at His feet as "the good part." He goes on to say that it "shall not be taken away from her." There is something about dwelling in God's presence that fills, satisfies, and changes a person eternally. Many of us are superficial in our hunger for God and are quite satisfied with just a tablespoonful of His mercy when He wants to pour out upon us the rivers of life.

Some never learn this crucial lesson. The next time we hear of these two dear sisters, the scene is much the same:

Jesus, therefore, six days before the Passover, came to Bethany where Lazarus was, whom Jesus had raised from the dead. So they made Him a supper there, and Martha was serving; but Lazarus was one of those reclining at the table with Him. Mary therefore took a pound of very costly perfume of pure nard, and anointed the feet of Jesus, and wiped His feet with her hair; and the house was filled with the fragrance of the perfume (John 12:1-3).

Martha was always busy, trying to find her fulfillment through the busyness of "serving the Lord." Mary chose the good part, fell at His feet, and worshipped Him. Who would you say was living in victory?

God has a universe full of need-filling mercies for you. But ultimately, they are all to be found in Him. As you learn to sit at His feet, drink in His beauty, bask in His love, and feel His compassion, every need of yours will be met—satisfaction guaranteed! Jesus tells us that our "Father knows what [we] need, before [we] ask" (Matthew 6:8). As we learn to take the Lord at His word we will learn how to rest in His bountiful provision and will truly enjoy His company. Only then will we discover the abundant Christian life and begin *living in victory*!

Bibliography

Chapter One
1. *Oswald Chambers, The Best From All His Books*, Thomas Nelson Publishers, Nashville, TN 1987; p. 223
2. Philippians 4:19
3. Robert Bolton as quoted by Iain H. Murray, *Jonothan Edwards, A New Biography*, Carlisle, Banner of Trust, reprint 1988; p. 128

Chapter Two
1. *Topical Encyclopedia of Living Quotations*, Bethany House Publishers, 1982; p. 117
2. *ibid*
3. *Topical Encyclopedia of Living Quotations, ibid*; p. 226
4. A.W. Tozer, *Jesus, Our Man In Glory*, Christian Publications, Camp Hill, PA, 1987; p. 84.

Chapter Three
1. Leonard Ravenhill, *Revival Praying*, Bethany House Publishers, 1962; p. 40
2. Andrew Murray, *In Search Of Spiritual Excellence*, Whitaker House, 1984; p. 116

Chapter Four

1. A.W. Tozer, *The Knowledge of the Holy*, Harper & Row Publishers, 1961; p. 103
2. Charles Finney, *Crystal Christianity*, Whitaker House, Springdale, PA 1985; p. 136
3. Andrew Murray, *Humility*, Fleming H. Revell Co., 1961; p. 10
4. Roy Hession, *The Calvary Road*, Christian Literature Crusade, Ft. Washington, PA; p. 17

Chapter Five

1. Joy Dawson, *Intimate Friendship with God*, Chosen Books, Old Tappan, NJ; 1986; p. 16
2. J.I. Packer, *Knowing God*, InterVarsity Press, Downers Grove, IL 1973; p. 30
3. Charles G. Finney, *Crystal Christianity*; p. 11
4. Colossians 1:10
5. Brother Lawrence, *The Practice of the Presence of God*, Whitaker House; 1982
6. *ibid*
7. *ibid*
8. *ibid*
9. Philip Yancey, *Disappointment With God*, Zondervan Publishing House, Grand Rapids, MI, 1988; pps. 92-93, 64
10. Alexander MacLaren as quoted in *The Bethany Parallel Commentary*, Bethany House Publishers, Minneapolis, MN; 1983; p. 198
11. A.W. Tozer, *The Pursuit of God*, Christian Publications, 1981; p. 17-18

Chapter Six

1. *The Quotable Lewis*, Tyndale House Publishers, Inc. Wheaton, IL 1989; pps. 408, 407, 405, 406
2. *God's Treasury of Virtues*, Honor Books, Tulsa, OK 1995; pps. 30-31
3. *The Zondervan Pictorial Encyclopedia of the Bible*, Zondervan Publishing House, Grand Rapids, MI, 1976; p. 183
4. QuickVerse Computer Program, Hebrew and Greek Dictionary extracted from the *Strong's Exhaustive Concordance of the Bible*,

Copyright 1980, 1986 and assigned to World Bible Publications, Inc.
5. *Vine's Expository Dictionary*, Fleming H. Revell Company, Old Tappan, NJ 1981; p. 116
6. *The Bethany Parallel Commentary of the New Testament*, Bethany House Publishers, Minneapolis, MN 1983; p. 1029
7. *The Quotable Lewis*; p. 292

Chapter Seven
1. Psalms 31:19; 36:5
2. *Baptist Hymnal*, Convention Press, Nashville, TN 1956; p. 47
3. The late James Thomas (who was a dear friend), *Mercy Truth and Judgment*; p. 4
4. *God's Treasury of Virtues*; p. 206

Chapter Eight
1. Mark 4:38
2. Habakkuk 1:2-3, 13
3. Revelations 14:19
4. *The Bethany Parallel Commentary of the Old Testament*; p. 1920
5. *ibid*
6. Catherine Marshall, *Beyond Our Selves*, McGraw-Hill Book Co., NY, NY; 1961; pps. 21-23.
7. *ibid;* p. 28

Chapter Nine
1. Psalm 139
2. Victor Ostrovsky & Claire Hoy, *By Way Of Deception*, St. Martin's Press, 1990; pps. 1-2
3. *ibid*; pps. 13-15
4. Hannah Whitall Smith, *A Christian's Secret of a Happy Life*, Whitaker House, Springdale, PA; 1983; p. 77. Used by permission.
5. H. D. M. Spence, *The Pulpit Commentary*, Vol. XI, MacDonald Publishing Company; pps. 444-445

Chapter Ten
1.*Oswald Chambers The Best From All His Books*; p. 223
2. *Topical Encyclopedia of Living Quotations*; p. 183

3. *ibid*; p.184
4. Hebrews 4:15-16
5. Steve Gallagher, *At the Altar of Sexual Idolatry*; pps. 136-137.
6. *Vine's Expository Dictionary*; p. 116
7. Spiros Zodhiates, *The Complete Word Study Dictionary*, AMG Publishers, Chattanooga, TN, 1993; pps. 1133-1134

Chapter Eleven
1. *God's Treasury of Virtues*; p. 278
2. Matthew 12:50
3. Rex Andrews, *What The Bible Teaches About Mercy*, Zion Faith Homes, Zion, IL; pps. 166, 3, 121
4. *Mercy Truth and Judgment*; p. 6
5. *A Christian's Secret of a Happy Life*; p. 42
6. *Oswald Chambers The Best From All His Books*; pps. 1-2
7. *A Christian's Secret of a Happy Life*; pps. 80-83
8. *What The Bible Teaches About Mercy*; p. 121
9. *Baptist Hymnal*; p. 356

Chapter Twelve
1. I John 2:17 KJV
2. Rosalind Goforth, *Jonothan Goforth*, Bethany House Publications, 1937; p. 109
3. Titus 3:14
4. *Baptist Hymnal*; p. 431

Chapter Thirteen
1. *God's Treasury of Virtues*; p. 47
2. *Oswald Chambers The Best From All His Books*; p. 320
3. *Jonothan Goforth*; p. 121
4. Matthew 5:6
5. These are available on audio and video tape through Heart Talk Ministry, 9616 Micron Ave. #900, Sacramento, CA 95827-2626

Chapter Fourteen
1. *Revival Praying*; pps. 64, 70
2. *ibid*; p. 14
3. Jack Hayford, *Prayer Is Invading The Impossible*, Ballantine

Books, NY, NY; 1977; p. 58
4. *ibid*; p. 49
5. *What The Bible Teaches About Mercy*
6. Andrew Murray, *The Ministry Of Intercession*, Whitaker House, 1982; pps. 138-139. Used by permission.

Chapter Fifteen
1. *Inspiring Quotations*; p. 215-216
2. *ibid*; p. 157
3. *ibid*
4. An Unknown Christian, *The Kneeling Christian*, Zondervan Book Publishers, 1971; p. 17
5. *The Bethany Parallel Commentary on the Old Testament*, p. 1015

Chapter Sixteen
1. Baker Book House, *The Best of C.H. Spurgeon*, Grand Rapids, MI, 1989; pps. 73, 75
2. Proverbs 16:6
3. *Oswald Chambers The Best From All His Books*; p. 328
4. *Topical Encyclopedia of Living Quotations*; p. 249

Chapter Seventeen
1. *Inspiring Quotations*; p. 76
2. *ibid*; p. 77
3. From the syndicated Ann Landers column, November 28, 1996
4. *Baptist Hymnal*; p. 260
5. Roy and Revel Hession, *We Would See Jesus*, Christian Literature Crusade, Ft. Washington, PA Copyright 1958; p. 26 Used by permission.

<u>Notes</u>

<u>Notes</u>

<u>Notes</u>

Pure Life Ministries

Pure Life Ministries helps Christian men achieve lasting freedom from sexual sin. The Apostle Paul said, "Walk in the Spirit and you will not fulfill the lust of the flesh." Since 1986, Pure Life Ministries (PLM) has been discipling men into the holiness and purity of heart that comes from a Spirit-controlled life. At the root, illicit sexual behavior is sin and must be treated with spiritual remedies. Our counseling programs and teaching materials are rooted in the biblical principles that, when applied to the believer's daily life, will lead him out of bondage and into freedom in Christ.

Biblical Teaching Materials

Pure Life offers a full line of books, audiotapes and videotapes specifically designed to give men the tools they need to live in sexual purity. You will find these teaching materials featured throughout this magazine.

Residential Care

The most intense and involved counseling the staff offers comes through the Live-in Program (6-12 months), conducted on the PLM campus in Kentucky. The godly and sober atmosphere at Pure Life Ministries provokes the hunger for God and deep repentance that destroys the hold of sin in men's lives.

Help At Home

The Overcomers At Home Program (OCAH) is available for those who cannot come to Kentucky for the live-in program. This twelve-week counseling program features weekly counseling sessions and many of the same teachings offered in the Live-in Program.

Care For Wives

Pure Life Ministries also offers help to wives of men in sexual sin. Our wives' counselors have suffered through the trials and storms of such a discovery and can offer a devastated wife a sympathetic ear and the biblical solutions that worked in their lives.

Pure Life Ministries
P.O. Box 410
Dry Ridge, KY 41035
(859) 824-4444—Office
(888) 293-8714—Order Line
info@purelifeministries.org
www.purelifeministries.org

OTHER BOOKS AVAILABLE THROUGH PURE LIFE MINISTRIES

AT THE ALTAR OF SEXUAL IDOLATRY

This book is for the everyday guy who needs real-life solutions. It draws back the curtain and exposes the inner workings of sexual sin in the heart, something Steve Gallagher understands: having lived in the bondage of it himself for over twelve years. Forget theories or opinions, this book imparts the biblical answers that have worked in his own life and in the lives of hundreds of men he has personally discipled since 1986.

SEXUAL IDOLATRY WORKBOOK ALSO AVAILABLE

The reader will have to dig for answers, both in At the Altar of Sexual Idolatry and in the Scriptures, which will help to cement biblical principles into his heart. Each chapter also includes questions especially tailored for weekly men's groups.

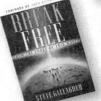

BREAK FREE *From The Lusts of This World*

We face perilous times – just as the Bible predicted we would. A demonic conspiracy is sweeping our nation, disseminating the deception that it is possible to live for the pleasures of this world without spiritual consequences.

At a time when the world is falling apart at the seams and all hell is breaking loose, God is looking for vessels willing to be set apart and filled with His anointing. Break Free from the Lusts of this World will increase your spiritual sobriety and prepare you for the soon to appear Day of the Lord.

THE WALK OF REPENTANCE

This 26-week Bible study has affected the lives of hundreds of people. Each week of this easy-to-use curriculum has a theme, addressing the challenges of the Christian life one step at a time.

Whether used by individuals, small groups, couples or even Sunday school classes, The Walk of Repentance makes a profound impact and leads sensitive hearts into a deeper intimacy with the Lord. Experience the times of spiritual refreshing that follow repentance; go deeper in God as you allow His Word to take root in your heart; find the freedom from sin enjoyed by those who walk in repentance!

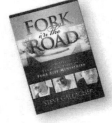

FORK IN THE ROAD

Stories From the Files of Pure Life Ministries

These eleven thought-provoking stories contain valuable life lessons for all Christians. Each of these people faced a life-defining moment at Pure Life Ministries, a time to make a choice for or against God, a choice that would inevitably alter the course of their lives. Grab a front row seat and take a peak inside the Pure life Ministries Live-In Program. Those who enjoy testimonies and stories will not only find this quick read a welcome edition to their library, but will be challenged to respond in the affirmative when they face their own Fork in the Road.

HOW TO RUN A SUCCESSFUL SUPPORT GROUP

There is a huge difference between an effective and powerful support group that brings real freedom and a poorly organized group of men sitting in a circle discussing their failures. This small book leads the new group leader step-by-step through the process of starting, promoting and running a group that will bring about changed lives.

TO ORDER: 1.888.293.8714 · *www.purelifeministries.org*